Wonderful
COUNSELOR

AND HE SHALL BE CALLED...

Wonderful
COUNSELOR

A FORTNIGHT *of*
CHRISTMAS MEDITATIONS

LARRY LIBBY &
STEVE HALLIDAY

WATERBROOK
PRESS

WONDERFUL COUNSELOR
PUBLISHED BY WATERBROOK PRESS
2375 Telstar Drive, Suite 160
Colorado Springs, Colorado 80920
A division of Random House, Inc.

ISBN 1-57856-315-1

Library of Congress Cataloging-in-Publication Data
Libby, Larry.
    Wonderful counselor : a fortnight of Christmas meditations / by Larry Libby and Steve Halliday.
        p. cm.—(And He shall be called)
    ISBN 1-57856-315-1
    1. Christmas—Meditations.   I. Halliday, Steve, 1957–   II. Title.   III. Series.
    BV45.L47 2000
    242'.335—dc21   00-042871
Printed in the United States of America
2000—First Edition

10 9 8 7 6 5 4 3 2 1

The magi were strangers and foreigners from Persia,
yet they came to see Him lying in the manger. Can you, a Christian,
not bear to give a brief measure of time to enjoy this blessed sight?
If we will present ourselves in a spirit of faith, there is no doubt
but that we shall truly see Him as He lies in the manger.
—St. John Chrysostom

CONTENTS

Introduction: The Best Thing About Christmas 1

1. Child of Wonder 7

2. A Counselor Like No Other 18

3. *One of Us* 30

4. Where God Hides His Gifts 38

5. Full of Grace and Truth 50

6. *A Tale of Three Unwise Men* 61

7. He Knows All 71

8. He Listens 86

9. *Simeon's Song* 95

10. "Do Whatever He Tells You" 104

11. Seeking God's Counsel 120

12. *The Counselor's Questions* 136

13. Infinite Supply 145

14. *The (Very) Best Christmas Pageant Ever* 158

THE BEST THING
ABOUT CHRISTMAS

*W*hat's the best thing about Christmas?

Is it the rich, pleasing sounds of old, familiar carols?

Silent night, holy night…

Away in a manger…

O little town of Bethlehem…

God rest ye merry gentlemen…

Each melody, each stanza, releases a sweet store of memory. We're carried back to other times and other places, with recollections of dear faces and well-loved voices and happy times together.

Is that the best part?

Maybe it's the scene of busy shops and city streets decked out in garlands of festive red and green. Or the delight of a small child enchanted by some wondrous, long-hoped-for toy. Or the majesty of a noble fir robed in hundreds of tiny lights, each one caressing in a soft, white glow the bright angel standing guard atop the tree.

Just what is the *best* thing about Christmas?

For those of us who love this season, the choices for "best thing" at first seem nearly endless. For celebrants with a sweet tooth, it may be freshly frosted cookies, sprinkled with colored sugar, consumed with a frosty glass of cold milk or mug of hot tea, just right for dipping or sipping. For the sociable, perhaps it's all the cards, notes, and letters from old friends, now scattered across the country. For moms and dads, quite possibly it's the holiday get-togethers that bring sons and daughters and grandchildren home from the far reaches of the earth.

All of these things give us great reason to celebrate, and all of them cheer our hearts. But in the deepest sense, only one thing truly qualifies as "best": Emmanuel, God with us.

What could ever compete with God's best gift to us? What could outshine the second person of the Trinity, Jesus Christ, who willingly left the glories of heaven to come to earth and become one of us so that He might redeem us from the miseries of sin?

Beyond all doubt, the best thing by far about Christmas

is that it commemorates the entrance of Jesus Christ into our fallen world.

Even so, you have to look for Him these days. He isn't as easy to spot as He used to be, even in the month of December. A politically correct culture has done its level best to erase His name from the cards, His glory from the music, His story from the schools, and His joyous reality from every public gathering.

But He's still here. Right where He's always been. History still turns on His advent and heaven still reaches out to lost, despairing men and women in His wonderful, life-giving name. And if we pay attention, the very best parts of our many yuletide celebrations still point us back, ever, always, to the Savior.

When we sing the old carols, we remember the hosts of heaven who with joy and wonder sang out the news of Christ's birth to Bethlehem's awestruck shepherds. When we see Ebenezer Scrooge turn from a "wrenching, grasping, covetous old sinner" into a "second father" for Tiny Tim, we remember that Jesus came to seek and to save that which was lost. When we nibble those snowman cookies, we remember the sweetness of our Lord. When we ogle presents under the tree, we remember God's great and unspeakable Gift to us. When we welcome home sons and daughters, we remember that our King is even now preparing a great banquet to which He will certainly welcome every one of His precious children.

During this joyful season, we offer the following meditations in the hope that their words might gently turn our thoughts to the Savior. It is our desire that *And He Shall Be Called…Wonderful Counselor* will help all of us to refocus on our magnificent Lord Jesus Christ, and to prepare our hearts for worship and adoration.

And make no mistake, preparation is essential.

The Magi likely had weeks, even months and years, to prepare for their famous audience with the newborn King. Might we not benefit from taking fourteen days—a fortnight—to consider the wonder of the One who came to save us? "The magi were strangers and foreigners from Persia," wrote John Chrysostom in the fourth century, "yet they came to see Him lying in the manger. Can you, a Christian, not bear to give a brief measure of time to enjoy this blessed sight? If we will present ourselves in a spirit of faith, there is no doubt but that we shall truly see Him."

Among all the rich possibilities for seeing Him, amid His varied roles, this little book of meditations turns the spotlight on the first of four momentous titles named in Isaiah's beloved passage:

For to us a child is born,

to us a son is given,

and the government will be on his shoulders.

And he will be called

Wonderful Counselor... (9:6, emphasis added)

All fourteen of the brief meditations that follow ponder the breathtaking benefits that are ours in this Wonderful Counselor. Together we'll ask, who is this Counselor? What are His qualifications? What kind of counselor is He? And how might He advise us this Christmas season?

Our proposal is a modest one. Read just one brief chapter a day for two weeks prior to Christmas Day. It really is a small commitment of time.

But with time comes focus.

With focus comes fresh truth.

With fresh truth comes wonder.

With wonder comes joy.

Keep in mind that although this work was prompted by a famous "Christmas text" and is meant to be read in the weeks before December 25, it's not your typical Christmas book. It doesn't focus on the glories of the season or of the holiday, but rather on the One who inspired both. We love what a celebrated English cleric wrote a century and a half ago: "To know Christ is life eternal. To believe in Christ is to have peace with God. To follow Christ is to be a true Christian. To be with Christ will be heaven itself. We can never hear too much about Jesus Christ."[1]

Jesus is the undisputed attraction here, and we've tried hard to find diverse ways to highlight His glory through both nonfiction and fiction. Fiction chapters are distinguished by italics in the table of contents and by the decorative border on each story. Chapters written primarily by Larry Libby are noted by his initials *(L.L.)*, while the initials *S.H.* indicate the work of Steve Halliday. Where no initials appear at the end of a chapter, it is a true team effort.

But enough of preliminaries. Join us now for a fortnight of encouragement and hope as we consider that most Wonderful of Counselors, Jesus Christ. May we all focus our hearts on Him during these few, quickly passing days, and revel in the wonder that He truly is—a wonder we will enjoy for all eternity.

---

1. J. C. Ryle, *Expository Thoughts on the Gospels* (London: J. Clarke, 1965), 2.

ONE

CHILD OF WONDER

And he will be called Wonderful...

ISAIAH 9:6

*T*he sounds and colors of Christmas have descended upon the wet, leaf-strewn streets and leaden skies of Portland, Oregon. Nat King Cole's velvet-toned "Christmas Song" pours from our office stereo like cream from a porcelain pitcher. In the little art studio across the street, someone perches on a stepladder to drape the large picture windows with banners announcing—what else?—a "HUGE" weekend Christmas sale.

Down the street, rosy-cheeked homeowners can be spotted hammering strings of lights to their eaves or attaching cutout Santas and reindeer to their chimneys. Just a few blocks from here, huffing shoppers scurry from store to store and sale to sale while mostly clueless part-time sales clerks keep asking the regulars how much is this and where can they find that.

If you were to ask all these rushing men and women what they thought of the season—if you inquired about "the meaning of Christmas"—you'd likely get a dizzying variety of answers. Everything from "love" to "presents" to "bowl games" to "a few days off work." And it's anybody's guess which name would pop up more often in your impromptu survey: "Santa" or "Jesus."

But how many of us ever get to the real *heart* of Christmas?

Yes, there's all the usual sparkle and glitz, music and mayhem—but how deep does it go? There are lights aplenty, but how much heat? How much passion? I can't help wondering. Is Christmas in America three thousand miles wide and a half-inch deep?

I'm reminded of a gift being hawked over the Net this year. It's called the "Virtual Fireplace." It's actually a six-hour video of a crackling fire in a traditional brick fireplace. The promotional ad on the producer's Web site boasts that it "turns your TV into an old-fashioned fireplace, perfect for relaxation or adding warmth to family gatherings."

Uh-huh.

One satisfied user writes, "The kids and I love to pretend that we are cuddling around a real fireplace." Another happy customer exults, "I have no fireplace in my home, and this video lets me bring a fireplace into almost any room in my home."

Who needs messy wood, hazardous matches, and environment-damaging smoke when you can cuddle up to your TV or computer screen, enjoying digitized flames in high-definition color and surround-sound? Quite an efficiency, wouldn't you say? Just flip a switch and there it is: all the brightness and pitch-popping delights of a blazing fire. No fuss, no muss, and costing only pennies a day to operate.

Never mind that it's two-dimensional.

Never mind that it produces neither light nor heat.

Never mind that it isn't real.

And never mind that the fire "captured" in such a video dwindled and died months—perhaps years—ago.

When I consider this popular stocking stuffer, I am reminded of our culture's frantic attempts to package Christmas while carefully avoiding the name of Jesus. The color is there. The sounds are right. And if you turn out the lights and squint across the room, you could almost pretend something's really there.

But it turns out to be only an illusion. There's no fire at all. A virtual Christmas—a Christmas without the burning, radiant centerpiece—has no power to warm a heart or fill a cold home with gladness and cheer.

But Jesus does.

And for those who truly know Him, there can be no question about "the meaning of Christmas." It isn't a day or a tradition; it isn't a square on a calendar or a yearly marketing opportunity.

Christmas is a Person.

A blazing, powerful, resplendent Reality.

And He is Wonderful.

A NAME FOR A NEWBORN KING

The prophet Isaiah placed the name "Wonderful," or in the original Hebrew, "Wonder," right at the beginning of his famous sentence to spotlight the preeminence of our Lord.

> For to us a child is born,
>> to us a son is given,
>> and the government will be on his shoulders.
> And he will be called Wonderful... (9:6)

The old prophet had seen it all. Or at least, he *thought* he had.

At times, Isaiah must have felt as if he'd already lived half a dozen lifetimes. He had seen four kings ascend to the throne of David while great and ominous events cast their shadows over the tiny kingdom of Judah. Massive world powers, bellicose and mighty, threatened a fragile and uneasy peace in the land of Abraham, Isaac, and Jacob. Competing ideologies vied for the hearts and minds of those who walked the streets of Jerusalem, the once-joyous but now greatly diminished capital of Solomon.

Isaiah was a husband and father, a brilliant writer, a statesman and patriot, a preacher and reformer, a theologian and teacher, and—last but not least—one of the mightiest prophets ever to lift his voice on Mount Zion. As God's spokesman to a disobedient nation, he'd been seized by vision after mind-numbing vision, delivering the messages with boldness and dignity into the often unwilling ears of kings and royal officials. The prophet had foreseen more action and drama than a roomful of Hollywood producers could have conjured in a decade.

Kings appointed and deposed.

Nations rising out of obscurity and falling into terrible ruin.

Fearful judgments and astonishing restorations.

Even the planet itself devastated and reborn.

Isaiah could certainly be excused for thinking he'd "seen it all." But he hadn't.

What God revealed to His spokesman in Isaiah 9 was more stunning than the movements of armies and empires.

Nothing, but nothing, captured this godly man's attention and set his pulse pounding like...*this*. It was staggering. Overwhelming. Exhilarating.

The vision made his fingers tremble and filled him with awe. As accomplished a writer as Isaiah certainly was, the astounding implications of that future event might easily have robbed him of words.

He needn't have worried. The prophetic utterance came pouring out of heaven like water from a broken levee, with one word overtaking all others.

Wonder.

"Wonder" is the name Isaiah gave to the One we know as Jesus Christ, the babe born in a manger who would become King of all. The prophet beheld His radiance, rising in the far-off future like a morning star, blazing with silver fire on time's shadowy horizon.

In the original Hebrew, Isaiah didn't use the adjective *wonderful* to describe this Child, but the noun *wonder*. "Not merely is the Messiah wonderful," wrote biblical commentator E. J. Young, "but He is Himself a Wonder, through and through."[1]

Today when you hear people use the word *wonder* at Christmas, they might be describing a dusting of snow on

---

1. E. J. Young, *Isaiah, Vol. 1* (Grand Rapids, Mich.: Eerdmans, 1965), 334.

the ground or the shimmer of tinsel or the twinkle of colored lights or the peal of faraway church bells. Truthfully, we have a rather weak concept of the term.

We grew up eating Wonder bread, reading Wonder Woman comic books, and contemplating Disneyesque images of Alice-in-Wonderland characters—mad hatters and talking rabbits. A generation of baby boomers grew up hating the old Lawrence Welk television program, where the North Dakota polka-king host used to croon, "Wunnerful, wunnerful," after practically every number.

These days, people use the word *wonderful* interchangeably with *nice.* You know, like warm milk and sugar cookies…or a nine-year-old picking out "Jingle Bells" on the family piano. Compared to the biblical description of *wonder,* our own definitions fade like the beam of a penlight at high noon.

So what is wonder? What is the genuine article? The wonder described in Isaiah 9 isn't some bland, bloodless adjective. It is a mountainous noun, soaring into the heavens like Everest, piercing the upper atmosphere. It isn't like plugging in the Christmas tree lights; it's more like grabbing a high-voltage power line straight out of Bonneville dam—powered by the majestic Columbia in full flood. This is a wonder that throbs with power, turns your knees to Jell-O salad, and prickles the hairs on the back of your neck.

Psalm 78:12 (NASB) uses the same root word to describe the miracles God performed in Egypt to rescue His people from slavery. Read the following description, and see if it matches up to some mild, greeting-card, Currier-and-Ives pleasantry…or if it shakes the very ground under your feet.

> He wrought *wonders* before their fathers,
> In the land of Egypt, in the field of Zoan.
> He divided the sea and caused them to pass through;
> And He made the waters stand up like a heap.
> Then He led them with the cloud by day,
> And all the night with a light of fire.
> He split the rocks in the wilderness,
> And gave them abundant drink like the ocean depths.
> He brought forth streams also from the rock,
> And caused waters to run down like rivers.
> (Psalm 78:12-16, NASB, emphasis added)

These earth-shattering events were seared into the consciousness of every true Israelite: The Red Sea split like a round of seasoned oak under a mighty ax…the pursuing armies of Pharaoh drowned within scant yards of fleeing Israel…a towering pillar of cloud and a resplendent pillar of fire led the people across a trackless wilderness. What a wonder!

And Isaiah chooses *that same potent word* to picture the coming Messiah. The prophet describes Him "not merely as someone extraordinary, but as One who in His very person and being is a Wonder; He is that which surpasses human thought and power; He is God Himself."[2]

ANGEL OF THE LORD

Jesus Christ always has been a Wonder. Many Bible scholars believe He visited earth many times before His birth in Bethlehem—in the form of a powerful angel…the Angel of the Lord.

In Judges 13:18, this Mighty One tells the farmer Manoah, "Why do you ask my name, seeing it is *wonderful?*" (NASB, emphasis added). In other words, "You can't even comprehend who I am. It is beyond your understanding."

Manoah might as well have inquired about the temperature at the core of the sun. He had no way of relating to something so vast, so impossibly distant from his experience.

Something of that awe clung to God's Son even when He clothed Himself in humanity. In one incident in the gospel of Mark we're told that "as soon as all the people saw Jesus, they were overwhelmed with wonder and ran to greet

2. Young, *Isaiah*, 334.

him" (9:15). When the mob came to arrest Jesus in the Garden of Gethsemane, His simple assertion "I am he" knocked the legs out from under them all (John 18:6). When the apostle John saw the living, resurrected Christ, "his face…like the sun shining in all its brilliance," he fell to the ground facedown (Revelation 1:16).

When we pause to think this Christmas about the One whose birth we honor, our spirits should soar to remember that He is not merely an infant lying in a stable, but God in the flesh—the greatest Wonder ever to visit this poor planet.

That's why it isn't feathery snowflakes, strings of lights, and aluminum stars that make the Christmas season "wondrous." The wonder isn't in well-loved traditions, family togetherness, celebrities donning fuzzy red hats, or some vague emotion of "goodwill."

The wonder is Him.

And it always will be.

MAKE HIM THE CENTERPIECE

Whatever joys or challenges we may face in the ragged rush of this season, whatever surprises or perplexities we may encounter, let us decide now, at the outset, to make *Him* the flaming heart of all our holiday celebrations.

After all, we enjoy a privilege unknown to Isaiah. He

could only peer through the murky currents and eddies of future days to catch a dim glimpse of this child who would be Wonder. Even so, the sight left him breathless and marveling.

Today we do not know Jesus merely as the fulfillment of a great prophecy but as our scar-bearing Brother, Savior, and King: It was He who came to earth and took on human flesh so that we might one day take on heavenly flesh and join Him in heaven.

So come to Him. Step into the warm embrace of God's eternal Son. There's nothing "virtual" about His power or His love.

He's real. He's like no other.

And He's the very definition of *wonder.*

A COUNSELOR LIKE NO OTHER

And he will be called Wonderful Counselor...

ISAIAH 9:6

*T*he comic strip universe just hasn't been the same since Ben Watterson retired from the playing field. No pen-and-ink creations—no matter how charming or wacky—have stepped forward to fill the sizable gap left by the irascible Calvin and his ever-faithful stuffed tiger, Hobbes...and I have a hunch none ever will.

I remember a strip from years ago when the irrepressible duo found themselves in a familiar pursuit—careening down a snow-covered hill on an out-of-control toboggan.

It always puzzled me how they managed to carry on calm, intelligent conversations while flying through the air at such amazing speeds and heading for such certain disaster.

"I've been good all day so far," Calvin notes.

"Christmas is getting near, huh?" asks Hobbes.

"You got it," Calvin replies, then continues. "I've been wondering, though. Is it truly being good if the only reason I behave well is so I can get more loot at Christmas? I mean, really, all I'm doing is saying I can be *bribed.* Is that good enough, or do I have to be good in my heart and spirit?"

The toboggan crashes wildly into a tree, launching the duo on a long arc through the winter sky to a snowy landing. Without missing a beat, Calvin pokes his head up through the snow and poses another question—and a rather weighty one at that: "In other words, do I really have to *be* good or do I just have to *act* good?"

Hobbes, gravely brushing snow from his orange and black stripes, declares, "I suppose in *your* case, Santa will have to take what he can get."

"Okay…" Calvin agrees, "so exactly how good do you think I have to act? *Really* good, or just *pretty* good?"

The spiky-haired little guy was looking for counsel. He didn't want generalities or broad-brush platitudes; he needed some specific information. After all, why exert himself to all that extra "goodness" if it didn't count for anything?

Calvin isn't alone in his desire for counsel at this time of year. The extra pressures and concerns—whether emotional or financial, physical or relational—press hard against us. Professional counselors will tell you that their schedules overflow at this time of year with troubled men and women desperately seeking to exorcise the ghosts of Christmas Past.

Where can we go to get the counsel we need? Check the Yellow Pages? Surf the Net? Ask our brother-in-law? Who's available at this hectic time of year? And even if someone actually had an open slot, who could begin to sort through the myriad complexities of our dilemmas?

So where do we turn for counsel? Whose wisdom can we trust?

In a time of national turmoil, the prophet Isaiah might have wondered the same thing. With binoculars provided by God's own Spirit, Isaiah looked down through the long years and caught a glimpse of Someone he could only describe as a Wonder. But as the image snapped into sharper focus, he saw not only a Wonder, he found himself looking into the eyes of a "Wonderful *Counselor.*"

IS HE *MY* COUNSELOR TOO?

What can such a phrase from so many centuries ago mean to you and me *today,* in the dilemmas and trials that assault our peace and erode our hope? Was the prophet simply heaping title upon title, honor upon honor to the majesty he saw from such a great distance? Or—could it be?—is this "Counselor" really Someone to whom you and I can turn in our distress and perplexity? After all, when you fall out of a ship on the high seas, you don't want someone to toss you a book of religion or philosophy, no matter how nice its cover and no matter how finely sculpted the pages. You need a life preserver! You need something to keep you afloat so that you're not drowned by the next salty wave that surges over you.

Does Jesus offer that kind of help?

One of my friends has a teenage son who had the misfortune to find himself in two noninjury car crashes in the days just before Christmas. Both were the young man's fault. Both seriously damaged his parents' second car. With the prospect of skyrocketing insurance rates prompting him to consider dropping some of his freshman college classes to find a job to pay for the mess, this young man swallowed a dose of distress as great as anything he'd faced in his young life.

My friend, however, can tell the story with a smile. After the second accident, his boy went immediately to his room, closed the door, sat on the floor by his bed, and opened his Bible. He didn't call his best buddy. He didn't even sit down with his parents to hash it out. He went right to Jesus, as fast as he could go. My friend, though not pleased that one of the family cars was out of commission, delighted in what that crisis revealed in his son's life. Running to the Wonderful Counselor in times of need is a habit that will sustain his son through *whatever* life throws at him.

I wonder, where do *you* go first when you need direction? Do you pick up a phone and call a friend? E-mail a sibling? Run to your pastor? Isaiah reminds us that the first and best place to go in a crisis is to our knees.

When you think about it, why go elsewhere? Why turn in another direction when such a matchless counselor invites us to take freely of the riches of His infinite understanding? Why not approach Him *first* for the insight we need at this—or any—time of year?

Isaiah wrote of Him: "Who has understood the mind of the LORD, or instructed him as his counselor? Whom did the LORD consult to enlighten him, and who taught him the right way? Who was it that taught him knowledge or showed him the path of understanding?" (40:13-14).

In other words, this is a counselor who doesn't need counselors. I could only shake my head to learn that a nationally known family counselor—a man who has written many books on personality and parenting—freely admits that he is in and out of therapy himself! Now, that could be a healthy choice for this man as he deals with issues from his past…but why would I go first to a man who has trouble dealing with *his own* personal struggles when a perfect counselor awaits my call?

Isaiah could have written many things about this Coming One. He might have called Him a wonderful warrior, for so He will be at the end of days. He could have called Him a wonderful moral teacher or a wonderful orator. But in God's plan, all of the wonder of this verse pours itself into that warm, approachable word: *Counselor.*

WHAT CAN I EXPECT?

What is a counselor? A counselor is a trusted friend who gives valuable insight. A godly thinker who directs our minds down pathways that please our Lord and bring release to our anxious hearts. A wise individual who can steer us away from foolish, unnecessary difficulties and guide us into wide, green pastures. In short, a good counselor is someone who has our best interests at heart *and who knows how to help us achieve those best interests.*

Has there been such a person in your past? Someone who placed a hand on your shoulder, looked at you with loving eyes, and spoke words of insight, affirmation—or even warning—into your ears?

Maybe it was a godly grandmother. A loving father. An older shipmate or army buddy who'd been there and back again. A wise and seasoned pastor. A professor who cared more about you than your grade in her class. You felt torn…low on hope…overcome with emotion…in way over your head…and this man or woman stepped into the gap with a warm, affirming touch and words that brought sanity and hope back to your wildly spinning world. You reached out—and someone grasped your hand.

One of the best counselors I've ever known was a man named M. R. Siemens. I met Dr. Siemens my sophomore year in college when I moved into 101 Summit Avenue, along with about twenty other student boarders. Dr. Siemens and his wife lived on one portion of the second floor of the sprawling home (formerly a frat house), while university students lived on floors one through three.

Dr. Siemens was a "retired" pastor who had been in the ministry for sixty years, ever since he'd turned sixteen years old. His six-foot-four-inch frame looked all the more imposing when he wore dark suits, which was most of the time. He had a rich, deep voice and a full shock of black hair. He frequently served as an interim pastor for wounded churches that had suffered a split or some other kind of trouble; people across the country knew him as someone who could nurse the injured back to health.

While Dr. Siemens might look and sound intimidating (especially when he drove his big Cadillac), he was one of the wisest and most gentle souls I've ever known. Many evenings I would appear at the door of his study as he prepared yet another local radio broadcast or sermon, and he'd invite me in for a long chat. I knew I could count on his counsel, whether it be a sound interpretation of some difficult Bible passage or a wise approach to some personal problem.

It was Dr. Siemens who counseled me to attend seminary and who suggested the school from which I eventually graduated.

It was Dr. Siemens who counseled me to accept people for who they were and who taught me to leave conviction to the Spirit.

It was Dr. Siemens who counseled me when I found myself caught in the middle of a personality clash between two strong ministry leaders.

It was Dr. Siemens who counseled me to use gentle humor to defuse potentially explosive situations.

It was Dr. Siemens who counseled me on the wisdom of stockpiling tactful responses to potentially troublesome encounters. (When some doting parents would present him with an especially homely infant, he'd break into a huge smile and say, "Now, *that's* a baby!")

I have no doubt that the reason he could so consistently offer such sound counsel was that He delighted to walk near to his Savior, Jesus Christ. His counsel reflected years of seeking the Wonderful Counselor Himself.

That's what Isaiah saw when he peeked through that gap in the curtain of time. A warm and wise personal advisor. A friend ready to sacrifice time and energy to help you and me sort through our troubles. Think of it! God Almighty willed from before the foundation of the earth that this child born in Bethlehem should counsel those who would otherwise die for lack of counselors. He is *our* Counselor given to help *us* in *our* perplexities and confusion.

And how we need Him! Even the best and wisest of this world's advisors encounter puzzles that leave them utterly baffled and abashed. They find themselves overwhelmed and outmatched by the intricacies and complexities that confront them. After their best efforts, they must walk away, knowing the knots remain tangled and snarled beyond their ability to untie them.

But the Son of God has never been daunted by any situation. No perplexities intimidate Him. No human difficulties tax His reasoning. As He told His disciples, "the Queen of the South…came from the ends of the earth to listen to Solomon's wisdom, and now one greater than Solomon is here" (Matthew 12:42).

And this advisor invites us to bring all of our perplexities, all of our puzzles, all of our doubts and fears and confusion to Him. When we stumble about in broad daylight; when the challenges of life leave us dumbfounded and groping for answers; when we do not know where to turn or what to do—Isaiah reminds us that we have a Wonderful Counselor who willingly takes us by the hand to show us the way out of our darkness and to illuminate our path through the blackest night.

THE WORD OF THE FATHER

When we take Jesus at His word and come directly to Him for guidance, we can be assured that He will speak nothing to us that the Father Himself has not already spoken to Him. "I do nothing on my own," Jesus said, "but speak just what the Father has taught me" (John 8:28). "My teaching is not my own," the Master insisted. "It comes from him who sent me" (7:16). Jesus' words are God's words. That means they can be utterly trusted, for God does not and cannot speak even the least false or misleading word.

Many years ago a trusted pastor and author wrote, "It is by the Word that God makes known His mind; and the Lord Jesus...came into this scene to make God known; in Him the Father has spoken out all that is in His heart. His words make known to us the path of life and show us the only safe way for us to travel through a world of sin."[1]

Who among us would not want to be shown "the only safe way...to travel through a world of sin"? And who wouldn't trust a counselor who knew that way—knew it

---

1. Harry Ironside, *Isaiah* (Neptune, N.J.: Loizeaux Brothers, 1949), 61.

forwards and backwards, inside and out, from the beginning to the end and from here to eternity?

Jesus is exactly that kind of guide, a counselor who invites you and me to come to Him for whatever we might need.

Even now.

At this very moment.

"Well," you might say, "I'm afraid you just don't understand. My situation is so tangled and confusing. There are so many layers to it, so many twists and turns, that I can't even explain it myself."

That may be. But you can't stump Jesus Christ. And if you will bring all the frayed edges, burned out wires, and splintered pieces to Him, He will begin to put your life back together. It's as simple as that.

"Yes," you say, "but I'm sure He has better things to do than concern Himself with this little problem of mine. He has given me many resources to deal with it, and I'm an adult. Surely He doesn't want me running to Him every time I get a little confused. No, I'll just handle this on my own."

That's an easy trap to fall into—the Israelites of Joshua's day could tell you just how easy. God had told them not to make a treaty with any of the people of Canaan, but some crafty men from Gibeon tricked them into just such a pact. By donning worn clothes and carrying moldy provisions of food they managed to convince Joshua's men that they had traveled a long distance—when in fact they were close neighbors. One sad passage tells the whole story: "The men of Israel sampled their provisions *but did not inquire of the LORD*. Then Joshua made a treaty of peace with them to let them live, and the leaders of the assembly ratified it by oath" (Joshua 9:14-15, emphasis added).

Not even the godly Joshua stopped to ask his Wonderful Counselor what *He* might think. And the result? The people fell into a great sin of arrogance that later would hound and ensnare them.

There's no reason we should repeat this ancient (and all too contemporary) mistake. When our Counselor invites us to come to Him for guidance, He puts no boundaries or limits on what we may ask. He says simply, "Come. Ask. Inquire. And let us enjoy this Christmas together as we have never enjoyed another."

What do you need to ask from this Wonder of a Counselor? What most troubles you this Christmas? What perplexes you? What problem seems insoluble, what difficulty seems insurmountable?

Whatever it might be, bring it to Him first. Lay it before His feet. Seek His counsel.

And discover for yourself why Isaiah called Him "Wonderful."

S.H.

THREE

ONE OF US

Since we, God's children, are human beings—made of flesh and blood—he became flesh and blood too by being born in human form; for only as a human being could he die and in dying break the power of the devil who had the power of death. Only in that way could he deliver those who through fear of death have been living all their lives as slaves to constant dread.

HEBREWS 2:14-15, TLB

Scene: A vast panorama of indescribable beauty—fading to places of empty whiteness, as a painting that is still unfinished— yet with enough detail here and there to awe the viewer with its splendor.

Angel: *[looking around]* I—I have never seen this place, Sovereign Lord. Not in all my travels. It overwhelms me.

Son: A work in progress, Zohar. No angel eyes have ever seen this place…until now. Come. Let us walk together awhile.

Angel: Ahh—such beauty! I fear it will consume me, Lord.

Son: Only with joy, Bright One. I wanted you to see it. It remains unfinished and yet, even now, it is good. It is a place I have been preparing.

Angel: Blessed One, may I ask for whom? Who will live in such a magnificent place?

Son: It is for My bride.

[The angel bows low in silence, until the divine hand lifts him again to his feet.]

Son: Come, let us walk. You wished to speak to Me, Zohar. What is on your heart?

Angel: Sovereign Lord…I would speak of a matter that lies close to the heart of *all* of us—every one of us in Flight 44.

Son: *[smiling]* You are elected spokesman again, Zohar? Your companions honor you greatly.

Angel: All honor to You alone, Lord. The others—well, they seem to will it so, Lord.

Son: As do I. Of course you may speak, Bright One. When has it been otherwise? I have ever delighted in your words and your service.

Angel: I hesitate, Lord, only because it concerns Your departure.

Son: Yes?

Angel: *[speaking quickly]* We are all consumed by it, Sovereign One, even if we seldom speak. You know all things, and I do not presume to imply that a Flight of simple angels could suggest anything that You have not already considered.

Son: Of course. But as I have said, I delight in your words. So speak, Bright One. Make your thoughts plain.

Angel: *[going now to his prepared speech]* Lord, we—the angels of Flight 44—we know that You know and weigh all things from eternity and…we further acknowledge there is much we fail to understand, though we long to understand more.

Son: Just as I have created you. But tell me your heart, Zohar.

Angel: Yes, Lord. But first I must say that I speak for us all. That is, for the whole Flight, Lord.

Son: Seven thousand of you. Worthy servants, all. I delight in each one.

Angel: Yes, Lord. Thank You, Lord. And here is the matter, Lord Most High. We wondered whether You might consider sending—one of us. *[hurriedly]* Any one of us would go to earth in a twinkling, Lord. There is nothing we would not do, no command we would refuse. We live to obey. We *delight* to obey.

Son: Yes, just as I have created you.

Angel: Our lives are many and are as nothing alongside

Yours. Why not—let one of us go in Your place? *Me*, for instance, or…well, any of us, for that matter. I would gladly lay down my life. So would we all.

Son: Ah, Zohar. But you know that you cannot lay down your life, except in service to your God—as you have already done since your eyes first opened. You are immortal. You could not die if you wished it. Even now, in another place, there are those who wish it and cannot. Have you ever heard of an angel dying?

Angel: Never. But if we *could* (and You could make it so), we *would*. Oh how we would! And Lord?

Son: Yes, Zohar?

Angel: Have not my brethren appeared in the form of men, Lord?

Son: Yes. As when two of your number accompanied Me to visit Abram and Sarai at Mamre.

Angel: Yes! We have sung of that day ever since. We sing every time it happens—every time one of us bears a message from You to the children of men.

Son: The singing of Flight 44 is known throughout the realms.

Angel: And all for You, my King. But here is my question. You *have* permitted us man-form, as it pleased You. So…why could not one of us appear in man-form

[33]

again and accomplish all You had planned? We can
appear in any form You command, can we not?

Son: "Appearing" in man-form is not what I intend,
Bright One. *[with quiet determination]* I will *become*
a man.

Angel: *[an involuntary shudder running through him]* Your
will is our food and drink, Lord, the very light of
our eyes. We only wish…we only wish there could
be another way. You know all things, Lord. Nothing
is impossible with You. We would not wish the Son
of the Most High to—well, of course *whatever* You
wish is what we wish, but—I have difficulty speaking this, Lord. You know my heart.

Son: I do.

Angel: *[chagrined]* I am not speaking at all well for my
companions.

Son: But you are, Zohar! You do well to yearn for My
honor. You do well to shrink from any thought of
your Lord suffering dishonor. I have created you for
such yearnings. They are as blood in the veins of a
man. Tell your companions, dear Zohar, that only a
man could pay for the sins of man. A *real* man,
Bright One. Not an angel in man-form, nor a man
in angel-form, nor an angel in angel-form. How
much do you know of man, Zohar?

Angel: As much as I am able to grasp, Sovereign One. I have studied under Gabriel. I have *seen* redeemed men—a few—at a distance. Father Abraham. Enoch. Rahab. The priest Zechariah has only recently come through The Gate. And, of course, Gabriel always speaks very highly of Daniel. We *all* want to make acquaintance of the redeemed ones. Very much so. There is—so much to ask. So much to understand. I would desire very much to speak to a man or, umm, to one of the other ones, a woman. But heaven is vast, and none have come—yet—to our sector. And we are all very busy.

Son: Heaven *is* vast, Zohar, but so is eternity! And the discoveries and the joys you will find there will never cease. In due time there will be occasion for all that your heart desires.

But on this other matter. Men do not spring to life, full grown, as you did. They begin as the smallest of seeds. They grow and take shape in the secret place and are born into their world. And so shall it be with Me. I will grow up in a home, with a dear human mother and a father-guardian. I will play with My companions in the sunlight. I will delight in the shaping of wood at the side of my father-guardian, Joseph, and my half brothers. I will taste of the bitter and the sweet. At the peak of My manhood, I will declare the eternal Kingdom to all who will listen. I will gather My scattered sheep back to the fold. And at the end, at the time appointed, I will lay down My life, suffering shame—and worse—bearing the sins of many.

Angel: *[in a whisper]* And so it must be?

Son: Yes, so it *will* be.

Angel: My Lord, You know that whatever God wills is what I will—with all my heart. Yet at the same time it tears at my heart.

Son: And Mine.

Angel: Then why, Lord? Why?

Son: *[with a gentle smile]* So that I may be all to them that they need. Lord. Counselor. Savior. Elder Brother. Friend. By which of those titles do you know Me, Zohar?

Angel: *[falling at His feet]* You are *Lord!* Lord of heaven. Lord of Lords. Lord of all!

Son: So I am. Yet these men and women and children whom I will buy with My own blood—they will also call Me Counselor and Friend. These, together, are My bride. And My Father will display the riches of His mercy to them so that all the hosts of heaven may marvel.

Angel: *[still on his face]* Amen! So be it, my King. I marvel even now.

Son: *[lifting the angel back to his feet]* Look around you, Zohar. It is the place to which I will bring My bride. In a day of distress, when darkness grows, I will come like a thief in the night to snatch her away. She will come to this place and be with Me forever. And when she comes, her garments will be white, with no stain or blemish. What a radiant bride she will be!

Angel: And that is why You must go? Why You must—die?

Son: Yes. And from that day on I will wear a human body, with scars in my hands and feet and side.

[The angel stands silent, looking for a moment at his own strong hands.]

Son: Yes, Zohar, I know. You would bear those for me as well, if only you could.

[The angel nods.]

Son: But I send you back now, angelic servant, flame of fire, back to your companions at Flight 44. Tell them to get ready to sing as they have never sung before. Tell them to polish their swords and brighten their raiment and prepare to outshine the very stars in the sky. They have a concert to give and they must be ready. Oh, Zohar! The shepherds will never forget this night!

FOUR

WHERE GOD HIDES HIS GIFTS

My purpose is that they may…have…complete understanding, in
order that they may know the mystery of God, namely, Christ, in
whom are hidden all the treasures of wisdom and knowledge.

COLOSSIANS 2:2-3

*I*t was a huge and delightful surprise, so tantalizing that
my middle brother, then just six years old, seemed thoroughly spellbound. I know household appliances don't normally capture the imaginations of active little boys, but you
have to understand that in those days our family finances
really needed to s-t-r-e-t-c-h. Oh, we got by just fine on my
dad's salary (I never remember going without anything), but
there was seldom room in the budget for extravagances.

Until that one particular Christmas.

That was the year Dad bought Mom a gleaming, brand-
new, black-and-gold Singer *sewing machine* from Mont-

gomery Ward—a present above and beyond all traditionally observed limits.

My father carefully hid the expensive gift away (probably in the attic; you had to clamber up there on a ladder and Mom rarely made the trip), and shared its secret with his two young sons, ages five and seven (I was only a baby at the time). The telling of the secret, of course, was accompanied by firm, clear instructions not to say *anything* about this to Mother until Christmas. Why? Because it was going to be a very big and wonderful surprise.

What happened next left such a mark in family lore that I heard about it years later. It's a tale lovingly repeated to this day.

One bright December morning my brother wandered into the kitchen. Seeing his mother at the sink, he was reminded of the Great and Marvelous Secret over which he had been given stewardship. How exciting it would be on Christmas morning! What fun it would be to see Mom gasp and clasp her hands in surprise! She'd probably cry, too. Girls were like that.

With a happy smile on his freckled face, he absent-mindedly sang a little tune he'd just made up, featuring those most memorable of lyrics, "O, sew-ing ma-chine, sew-ing ma-chine"—until he looked up and saw Mother looking down at him with a curious look on her face. Instantly realizing the enormity of his blunder, he paled, clasped a hand over his mouth, and ran from the room. Ah, but the cat had escaped the proverbial bag. Mom would still revel in her precious gift on December 25, but the Big Surprise that was to accompany it would be long gone.

SWEET SURPRISE

Why do we so enjoy hiding away the treasures we plan to spring on those we love the most? What is it about surprising our loved ones with unexpected gifts that causes our pulses to pound, our faces to beam…and sometimes, our tongues to wag?

A surprise gift, I suppose, is a way of saying "I love you" with an action rather than just words. It's a way of making love visible—of investing it in a tangible, touchable, wrappable something that we can place into the very hands of our friend or loved one. By it we say, "This is something I wanted for you, because you mean so much to me."

I think that's true of our God, as well. The Bible says He also hides treasures away—more plentiful than we could ask or imagine. In fact, "No mere man has ever seen, heard or even imagined what wonderful things God has ready for those who love the Lord" (1 Corinthians 2:9, TLB).

With all of time and the whole universe at His disposal,

God could find some pretty amazing hiding places to tuck away such surprises. (You won't catch me probing around the sizzling craters of Mercury or peering into the icy canyons of Pluto!) And yet in His wisdom and sovereignty, He has chosen to hide *all* the secrets of wisdom and knowledge in just one place.

They're all in His Son, Jesus.

Every one of them.

That's the bold, sweeping claim made by the apostle Paul, who wrote to the Colossians: "My purpose is that they may…have…complete understanding, in order that they may know the mystery of God, namely, Christ, in whom are hidden all the treasures of wisdom and knowledge" (Colossians 2:2-3).

Jesus Christ, our Wonderful Counselor, is the very source of wisdom and knowledge. You needn't look for these treasures under beds or in hidden boxes in the basement. They are in Jesus. All of them. Right now and forever.

And they are for you.

But isn't it interesting, this phrase the apostle chose? The precious *treasures* of true wisdom and knowledge are *hidden* in the Son of God. I read mystery in that statement. I sense the excitement of tucked-away boxes and delicious surprises.

When Paul uttered these words, he was seeking to make a point with some misguided believers who were looking for treasure in all the wrong places. The Colossians had become enamored with so-called spiritual teachers who boasted visions of angels and special insight into divine mysteries. "Don't believe it!" Paul exhorted. "Don't become diverted! You don't need intermediaries. You don't need to be spoon-fed by religious philosophers or bleary-eyed spiritual gurus. You just need Jesus—and as much of Him as you can beg, borrow, or steal."

That's important to remember at Christmastime, when we're surrounded by gifts and preoccupied with keeping them hidden. During this season of happy secrets and special presents, it's especially appropriate to recall that the biggest and best treasures of all are hidden safely away in our Lord Jesus, ready to be presented and unwrapped at just the right moment. During the yuletide season, it's good for us to reflect on what's *really* precious.

My mind goes back a couple of summers ago to the day my son Matt and I launched out on our first backpacking trip into the Oregon Cascades. We quickly realized that water was a major issue. At home or at work, you don't think much about water. You just stroll over to the tap or drinking fountain, let the cool stuff slide down your throat, and go on your way. You just do it—without really thinking about it. Up in the mountains, however, when the August sun is scorching your scalp and you're sweating under the weight of a fifty-pound pack, the subject of water is never very far from your thoughts. *How much is left in my canteen? Am I drinking enough? Am I carrying too much? Where is the next stream?*

When we found such a stream, even though the water looked crystal clear, we took special precautions, making use of water purification tablets. Why? Because you never know what kind of critters have been in that water upstream (or what they might have been doing there). One time, however, we came to a place where icy cold water bubbled right out of the rock, pooling up and forming a little stream. Slipping off our heavy packs, we knelt and drank directly from the spring.

Ahh, sweet ecstasy! No drink in the world—soft, hard, or otherwise—could match the taste of that pure water, right out of the icy veins of the mountain.

That's what Paul was telling the Colossians. "Why in the world would you want to drink downstream, ingesting water that may well be contaminated? Why drink suspect, polluted water when you can go freely to the very headwaters and plunge your face into the icy sweetness that bubbles right out of the Rock?" The book of Colossians fairly shouts the message. Drink your fill of Christ! Drink until you can drink no more. Drink until your water-starved tissues are replete with Him. Then, for the rest of your life, never stray very far from the Source. It will become for you as "streams of living water" flowing from within (John 7:38).

All of the treasures of life are in Him.

All the gifts of a generous and extravagant Father are in Jesus.

Don't waste your time looking anywhere else.

DESPERATE FOR HIS WISDOM

Have you ever found yourself as desperate for knowledge and wisdom as a thirsty man is for water? When you're really, *really* thirsty (I've been there at least once in my life), you want a drink more than anything else. You can't be tempted by offers of steak dinners, candy bars, or cherries jubilee. You want one thing and one thing only.

When you need advice, when crucial, life-impacting issues are at stake, you want the wisdom of the Lord. Nothing else will suffice. It is this treasure you seek; no other riches will do.

Just give me the wisdom of God.

Just give me the Wonderful Counselor.

Once you have tasted of *His* wisdom, once you have felt the touch of His directing hand, nothing else in the wide universe will do. He is "the LORD Almighty, wonderful in counsel and magnificent in wisdom" (Isaiah 28:29). To Him "belong wisdom and power; counsel and understanding are his" (Job 12:13).

I remember feeling an overwhelming desire for the Lord's wisdom as a young man, about to take what seemed a frighteningly large step. I was intending to ask Laura (now my wife of twenty-two years) to marry me. I'd counseled with my pastor, I'd counseled with my parents, I'd counseled with my boss, and I'd counseled with my friends. I was up to my ears in good advice.

But it wasn't enough.

Man, oh man. This was *marriage.* This was for keeps. I wanted to hear from God.

On a Saturday morning in June, I left my little apartment on the east side of Portland, Oregon, and walked up to Mount Tabor Park, a large wooded area on an extinct volcano within the city limits. With my little New Testament tucked in my hip pocket, I climbed up on the east slope of the hill, as far away from people and cars and traffic as I could get. And I poured out my heart to my Lord Jesus all day long.

Did He want me to marry? Was it the right time? The right girl? The right circumstances? The right reasons? Was there any reason why I shouldn't? Were there hidden dangers? Would I be missing some other purpose or opportunity He might have for me if I went that direction? I read my testament. I talked out loud. I prayed. I wept. And I listened. I wanted the wisdom of Christ more than anything else. Any other counsel at that moment would have seemed utterly irrelevant and unwelcome.

Talk to a psychologist? *Why?* Call Rush Limbaugh or Dr. Laura for life direction over the airwaves? *No thanks.* Write to Dear Abby or some other advice columnist? *Not a chance.* Consult a horoscope? *Uh-uh.* I wanted the treasures of heaven—wisdom and knowledge—and nothing else really counted.

Why would I have been so unsatisfied with any other counsel? Because I had tasted the counsel of God in my life. I had experienced the presence of Jesus, the Wonderful Counselor, and all other counsel seemed like so many little slips of paper stuffed into a fortune cookie.

The apostle Peter expressed similar sentiments in the gospel of John. There came a time when the twelve disciples had the option of continuing to walk with Christ or turning their search for meaning in another direction. Jesus, knowing in His heart that many of His followers were little more than superficial groupies, challenged them with some teaching that rocked them in their sandals.

"On hearing it," Scripture says, "many of his disciples said, 'This is a hard teaching. Who can accept it?'" (John 6:60). In other words, "This doesn't fall easily on our ears. This isn't what we expected. This isn't what we wanted to hear. This isn't popular or palatable or culturally acceptable.

What He's saying makes us uncomfortable, and we don't *like* to be uncomfortable. This isn't the kind of inspirational teaching we've been accustomed to. We don't need this."

John tells us that "from this time many of his disciples turned back and no longer followed him" (6:66). As Jesus watched them walk into the distance, talking and gesturing among themselves, he turned to the twelve who stood beside Him.

In so many words, He said, "All right, guys. What about you? Is this teaching too hard for you? Are you, too, going to bail on Me?"

Peter put his answer into words that would be true for any one of us. "Lord, to whom shall we go? You have the words of eternal life. We believe and know that you are the Holy One of God" (6:68-69).

In other words, "What else is there? We're ruined for anything else. We've burned all our bridges. We've chucked all the old ways and trashed all the bromides. If You're not the answer, then there is no answer. But since You *are* the answer, You're all we want. Just You. Forever."

But Peter, we might ask, *don't you find the words of Christ…um, a little difficult to understand?*

"Yeah. Honestly, yes. That part about eating His flesh and drinking His blood (6:53-56)? I don't get it. The truth is, I don't get what He's saying about half the time—and the other half of the time I'm only half sure. But I know this. Jesus has the words of eternal life. He's the Holy One of God. He's all there is. I don't care if His words are hard or soft, difficult or easy, harsh or comforting, puzzling or crystal clear. I don't care if He pats me on the back with them or clubs me alongside the head. His words are *true,* and I won't have any other."

Amen, Peter. Once you've tasted the counsel of Christ, all other counsel is as insipid as cold Cream of Wheat, minus the salt. The treasures of wisdom and knowledge are in Him alone.

CHRISTMAS EVERY DAY

Once my wife and kids and I have opened our gifts on Christmas morning—no matter how precious those unique little treasures and fancy treats might be—we're finished. No more presents. That's it. There's a big empty place under the tree, all of that wrapping we labored over is in the trash can…and we might find ourselves feeling just a little bit empty or blue.

Thank God it's never like that with the infinite treasures of wisdom and knowledge hidden away in Christ Jesus. You never know when He might take a radiant jewel of wisdom out of hiding here or select a present out of storage there—

and surprise you with it when you're not even looking. For what reason? Just because He loves you and wants you to know it.

The counsel of Jesus will never run out, because His treasures of wisdom and knowledge remain as rich and full today as they were in the days of Adam. His stash of gifts can never be depleted!

In a way, God treats every day as if it were Christmas. No matter the date on the calendar, He keeps dispensing treasures that, until that moment, were hidden away in Christ.

No matter what the gift, it will always fit you to perfection. It will be the right color, the right style, and the right flavor to meet the very need of the moment. How could it be otherwise, coming from the hand of One who has known you since before the world began?

L.L.

FIVE

FULL OF GRACE AND TRUTH

The Word became flesh and made his dwelling among us. We have seen his glory, the glory of the One and Only, who came from the Father, full of grace and truth.

JOHN 1:14

*W*ho is this Son of God who clothed Himself in human flesh? What is He all about? What is He like?

John, who knew Him as well as anyone, groped for words. Given the limitations of language—even a language as precise as Greek—the old fisherman put it as plainly as he knew how.

"I'll tell you this," said John, *"He is full of grace and truth."*

That's the kind of counselor and friend I want in my life. I desperately need truth, yes. Without it—without guardrails and bright, clear striping down the center of the highway—I will end up in a ditch. (I know me!) But I can handle only so much truth at a time; give me too large a dose in one shot and I will crumple like a plastic cup in the campfire.

So I desperately need grace, too. Without it, I will simply shrug my shoulders and give up. (I know me!) But grace without truth is like a heater in a car without wheels, sitting up on blocks in the carport. It comforts me and keeps me warm, but I don't *go* anywhere.

Years ago a friend and I met regularly to discuss "accountability" issues over breakfast. We were both young fathers and both struggling with particular ongoing problems. Every Saturday we would meet, load up on cholesterol and caffeine, and talk about our walk with Christ. Inevitably defeat would creep into our conversation, like fog curling up from the ground. We would accept one another, "encourage" one another to seek God's forgiveness and grace, then go home and promptly repeat the same sins through the following week…week after week. We were accommodating, we were friendly, we were sensitive, we were oh-so-encouraging…and we were going absolutely nowhere.

We met for two years. *Two years* of Saturday mornings. And I can't say either of us grew even a spiritual millimeter during that time.

How I wish I could retrieve and relive those Saturday mornings! In retrospect, I wish my friend would have grabbed me by the shoulders and said, "Hey, reality check! How long is this going to go on? I like eggs 'n' hash browns as well the next guy, but what are we doing here? Are we just playing tiddlywinks for the rest of our lives, or do we really want to become men of God? Let's get with it or just bag the whole thing! Tell you what. I'm going to call you every day, get in your face, and challenge you to keep your commitments—and I want you to do the same for me. The Bible says God has given us all we need for life and godliness. Let's get after it, man!"

That's what we should have said to one another. But we didn't. We had a lot of grace, but truth was scarce in our relationship. Since I moved from that city, we don't even keep in touch anymore. Each of us, I imagine, reminds the other of that dismally stagnant period of life in our thirties...and oh-so-many missed opportunities.

In all our Bible studies together, we somehow missed the truth of Psalm 141:5: "Let a righteous man strike me—it is a kindness; let him rebuke me—it is oil on my head. My head will not refuse it."

The kindest thing I could have done for my brother (and he for me) would have been to "strike him" with truth. To rattle his teeth a little. It was unkind and ultimately unloving of me to allow that situation to drag on for two empty years.

THE HARD SIDE

When Jesus spoke, both grace *and* truth were always present. The disabled, the discouraged, the disenfranchised, the down-and-outers, and crowds of little children grabbed every chance to be near Him, because He was so gracious, winsome, and kind.

Yet He did not shrink from rattling teeth.

To the Pharisees and teachers of the law who angrily rejected His grace and dragged to hell with them as many of their countrymen as possible, there was nothing left but hard truth: "You snakes! You brood of vipers! How will you escape being condemned to hell?" (Matthew 23:33).

To those who had turned the holy courts of the temple into a Wal-Mart parking-lot sale, He delivered the truth with unaccustomed force, overturning their benches and tables. "Is it not written: 'My house will be called a house of prayer for all nations'?" He shouted. "But you have made it 'a den of robbers'" (Mark 11:17).

To those who followed Him looking for shallow excitement or a free meal, He declared hard teachings until most of them became disillusioned and walked away.

Even to His dear friend Peter, Jesus spoke hard truth: "Get behind me, Satan! You are a stumbling block to me; you do not have in mind the things of God, but the things of men" (Matthew 16:23).

That's the kind of counselor He is and always will be. With Jesus you can always count on truth, and you can always count on grace. He tells you the truth—the whole truth—about your life and your situation, then He sticks with you come hell or high water.

He is the doctor who diagnoses your leukemia, then gets on the table next to you to donate his own blood and bone marrow.

He is the judge who pronounces a stiff fine and jail sentence, then cashes in his own 401(k) to pay your fine, stands by your family, and visits you every day in prison.

He is the man at the gas station who shakes his head sadly, tells you that you're many miles off course, then crawls into his own pickup to lead you through a nightmare maze of streets in the dark and the rain, all the way to your destination.

He is truth. He is grace.

In His truth, He tells me the real story about my life and where I stand. He tells me I am spiritually dead, booked on a one-way flight to hell, incapable of achieving heaven on my own power, incapable of lifting myself out of the despair of an empty life or releasing myself from the iron chains of habitual sin. In His grace, He loves me, seeks me, calls me, redeems me, walks with me through the hours of the day, and stands guard over my slumber at night.

He loves me enough to tell me the truth. But then in unmerited, undeserved, incomparable kindness, He offers Himself as the penalty my sin deserves and allows me to receive His righteousness.

NO MORE THAN WE CAN BEAR

After surgery on my right arm this past summer, I was required to go through a regimen of physical therapy to regain the use and strength of the damaged muscles. First, the therapist had me doing arm movements with nothing in my hand. That accomplished, he had me gripping a soup can, hoisting it up and down, back and forth. From there, I graduated to daily Thera-Band exercises—making use of those thin strips of stretchy material that you're supposed to tie to a door knob, pulling, pushing, and twisting until you've thoroughly exercised your protesting muscles. I began with a yellow (easy) Thera-Band, then stepped up to the intermediate ranks with a red one. From here, I'm told, I'll soon be working with a studly green band. And where from there? Bending steel bars with my bare hands, maybe? The point is, a therapist is trained to know how much a damaged muscle or joint can bear. His or her aim is to slowly strengthen that limb as it heals.

Jesus is *that* sort of counselor—a counselor who knows precisely how much you can bear and will not exceed that burden. Just before He went to the cross, with His remaining time on earth evaporating like water on a hot sidewalk, Jesus had much to tell His disciples. But His men simply had no capacity to hear it. Their hearts were confused, shaken, and weighted with sorrow.

"I have much more to say to you," He told them, "more than you can now bear. But when he, the Spirit of truth, comes, he will guide you into all truth" (John 16:12-13).

Isn't that beautiful? He's saying, "Dear friends, My heart is full of truth—and how I long to impart it to you. But I know you can't take it all in right now. You can't handle it. So I'm going to give it to you piece by piece, little by little through the years—in just the right places at just the right moments."

Thousands of years before Jesus was born, the prophet Isaiah looked down through the long years and saw this aspect of His ministry.

"Here is my servant, whom I uphold,
my chosen one in whom I delight…

He will not shout or cry out,
     or raise his voice in the streets.
A bruised reed he will not break,
     and a smoldering wick he will not snuff out."
     (42:1-3)

Have you ever been a bruised reed? Have you ever felt so weak and depleted that a puff of wind could just blow you over? Jesus is the perfect counselor for you. Weak as you may be, He will never break you beyond repair. In fact, He will strengthen and support you while you heal.

Have you ever felt like a smoldering wick on a candle? As though one crossly spoken word could just snuff you out? Jesus is a counselor who will keep your flame alive. No matter how the winds may howl around you, He will shelter you with His own hand.

HOW MUCH IS TOO MUCH?

It takes a wise counselor to know how much is enough and how much is too much. I struggle with that sort of wisdom as a parent. At times I have closed my eyes to situations that needed the hard edge of truth. Other times I have unloaded a whole dump-truck load of truth on a bruised reed.

I can't help but remember my own father's example at

what might have been a turning point in my life. I came out of a groggy sleep one Saturday morning to see my dad sitting beside my bed.

I groaned out loud.

"So...I see you're pretty sick," he said.

"Yeah."

When had I ever been sicker? When a fourteen-year-old boy who's seldom even tasted alcohol guzzles as much malt liquor as he can hold at one sitting, it tends to work a hardship on the body.

"That stuff—it's like poison, son. It can kill you."

I didn't know if he meant physically or morally, so I remained silent.

So did he. For a long time.

I knew he was filled with grief. I knew he was trying to think of something to say. It was the first "real trouble" I had ever given my parents—I, the young man who loved church, loved youth group, and loved the Lord.

But for whatever reason—curiosity, excitement, peer pressure—I had decided to see what it would feel like to be drunk. I found out. Boy, did I find out. I never even knew I had such a thing as liver bile until that terrible night.

My dad cleared his throat. I braced myself, weak as I was. Whatever he said to me would be deserved. Whatever tongue-lashing I received would be less scathing than the self-loathing I already felt.

"What happened to the kid we thought we could trust?"

With that, he got up and left the room and—perhaps sensing that I'd already learned a hard lesson—*never said anything about it again.* But, oh, the pain of that moment! I'd let my dad down. I had disappointed and grieved him. To this day it makes me wince to remember. A beating would have been easier to bear than those ten quiet words from the man who sat at my bedside. That question was like a sword thrust.

I heard the back door close. Weakly, I roused myself to look out my bedroom window. Dad was out in the backyard, at the picnic table under the cherry tree. He was studying his Sunday school lesson in preparation for teaching the ninth-grade boys. My class.

I washed my face, walked woozily out to the backyard, and sat on the picnic table across from him. The summer wind rustled the leaves of the cherry tree. I had grieved my dad, but I wanted to be near him, as close as I could get. His good and righteous life drew me. His decision to simply express his sorrow, rather than raking me over the coals or lecturing me, broke my heart. I loved this man and wanted to be like him. I still do. Through the years he had given me a great deal of truth. But in that moment, he sensed I didn't need more "truth"...just a glimpse of his heart...just a word of grace.

Jesus is that kind of counselor. He won't make excuses for your sins, pigeonhole you as a helpless "victim," or paint over your moral failures with a glaze of psychobabble.

He will tell you the truth.

He will bring you to your knees.

He will break your heart precisely where it needs to be broken.

Then He will wrap a strong arm around your shoulders and stay with you every waking moment until you step through the gates of His Father's house.

Christmas reminds us of our Wonderful Counselor's perfect ability to tell us the awful truth while upholding us with His grace. At Christmas, as we celebrate at the manger, we are awed by the grace of God's gift of His Son. But we also are reminded of a terrible truth: Because of our sin, He came to die. For us.

That's grace.

That's truth.

And without both working together, we would have neither.

L.L.

SIX

A Tale of Three Unwise Men

They…did not wait for his counsel.

PSALM 106:13

*G*reat constellations! Aren't you two ready *yet?*"

Already fifty-seven minutes late for departure by his reckoning, Gaius glared at his two companions.

"Come *on!* I've had word they'll be leaving anytime now, and then we'll have wasted our advantage. What is *keeping* you? How much gear do you think we'll need, anyway? We're bound for Palestine, not Egypt!"

Blastus said nothing, but looked up at his leader with the same tired, drooping expression that always hung from his weary face. A quiet, nearsighted man who loved poring over maps and charts of the heavens from a distance of an inch from his nose, he traveled only with great reluctance.

Malchus, the third of the party, ventured to speak.

Peering around his half-loaded camel he said in a soft, well-modulated voice, "Gaius, it grieves us to see you worked up into such a lather over this departure. Neither Blastus nor I have your energy, and to be honest, I'm still wondering if we're not heading off on this adventure a little too hastily. Wouldn't it be better if we simply joined our brothers' caravan? They have graciously invited us and—"

"Enough!" Gaius cut him off with a snarl. "We've gone over this too many times already. Why should we share the glory with *those* three? I'm sick to death of hearing about the three golden boys, following yonder star. You'd think they were the only Magi in town. Well, we know the stars too. We studied under the same masters as they did, and we have everything we need to get the job done. We don't need those three condescending glory-grabbers—or their fabled wisdom, either." Gaius spat, slapping his camel on the rump in frustration. The camel squawked in surprise and spat back, barely missing its target.

"Bah!" Gaius continued. "How hard could it be? Our maps and star charts are identical to theirs. Let's just get on the road, and we'll figure out the details once we get there."

"But I'm so tired," Blastus said meekly. "Couldn't we wait at least until morning?"

"NO!" Gaius roared, startling Blastus's mount and nearly sending its sleepy rider tumbling to the sand below.

Disregarding his friend's precarious position, Gaius persisted. "Starlight and moonbeams! I just explained all that. We *have* to get there *first*. This is our chance, our moment. Do you want the history scrolls to remember *them* as the Magi who found the King of the Jews? We dare not delay. Now get down off of that beast and help Malchus load up. Yes, Blastus, my nearsighted friend, I mean you. Pick up those gift boxes of gold, frankincense, and pomegranates. If you two aren't ready in ten minutes, I'm leaving without you— and I'll have the history scrolls all to myself."

Mile after sandy mile, day after blistering day, the trio's long journey unfolded. Field and fountain, moor and mountain, Blastus, Malchus, and Gaius hurried westward to their hoped-for date with destiny, stopping only briefly for rest and supplies. Through the difficult weeks the three friends often reprised their initial conversation: Blastus complaining of weariness; Malchus despairing over their "hasty" journey and berating himself for going along with such folly; and Gaius alternately urging his friends on to imagined acclaim and raking them savagely for their measured, unhurried pace.

And so it went, until one day a large city loomed on the horizon. Gaius was sure they had arrived.

"There it is!" he yelled, sitting up on his mount and

pointing excitedly to the massive walls rising in the distance. "On that hill! That's the place, all right, or I'm a Persian rug! We made it! Ha-ha! And we made it *first!* No sign of the golden boys at all!"

His companions fell silently into line behind Gaius as he urged his long-suffering camel toward the city gate. Merchants rushed out to meet the men as soon as they recognized the trappings of foreign wealth, but Gaius waved them away. He knew enough of the international trading language to discourage any hope of a quick profit at their expense.

"Be gone, riffraff! We have a *king* to locate!"

"There is the great palace," said Malchus. "Let us seek out one of their officials and see what may be learned."

"Never!" snapped Gaius. "We can't let these Hebrews think we Easterners don't know what we are doing."

"Which is all too true," muttered Blastus beneath his breath.

"What was that?" Gaius demanded, his head snapping back.

"I said, *'Good for you,'* O wise one. Do you think these foreigners have such a thing as an inn with a bit of liquid refreshment?"

Malchus, undaunted by his leader's lack of response, noted, "Well now, there is a lovely temple before us. Let us consult the priests. Do you suppose these Jews remember the God of Daniel, the illustrious founder of our order?"

A withering glance choked off Malchus's words.

"We…can…handle…this…by…ourselves," Gaius seethed through clenched teeth. "Are we Wise Men, or common tourists? Let us begin our search of the city."

As Blastus swayed woozily on his camel, Gaius gave a yank on the reins and resumed his parade through the streets, followed by a skittering army of ragamuffin children. Malchus sighed deeply. It was obvious there would be no further discussion.

Three days later—weary, utterly fruitless days—not even Gaius could ignore the buzz sweeping through the city. Young men and old women, traveling merchants and shopkeepers, the rich and the poor alike all seemed to be greatly agitated. Since none of the three friends understood much of this strange tongue, they could grasp little of the significance of the news. But at last they managed to decipher at least this much: the arrival of some important foreign dignitaries in costly raiment had caused the local king (and his subjects) no little distress. Beyond that they could understand nothing.

But it was enough.

Gaius realized his worst fears were coming true.

"Friends," he said, desperation in his voice, "we must

hurry! This can only mean that *they*—the usurpers—have been here. Ah me, had we not dawdled in the desert we would have reached our goal. But now? Now we must find out where they are—and where they are headed. Haste, friends, haste!"

"Haste?" asked an incredulous Malchus. "We have been rushing around this city for three days, chasing shadows and ghosts. Despite our pleas, you have been unwilling to find a local priest who might be able to inquire of Daniel's God—and who else placed that great star in the sky?—to help us on our way. We might have been given the answers we seek. But no. Here we are, and our more sensible brethren have obtained the information they need and are off on a great adventure. And you want *haste?* To where, pray tell, do you propose to hasten?"

Gaius glared at Malchus and ignored his question with a lordly sniff. "We can still fulfill our destiny, my friends," he declared. "We have suffered a setback, but no more. What matters is our mission. We must find our rivals and beat them to the goal. Nothing else matters."

Grim-faced and determined, Gaius set his gaze forward and spurred his mount on—but to where? He did not know. Nor did he try to find a priest. After another futile day of wandering the confusing city, trying to communicate in the little merchant tongue he knew, Gaius discovered to his deep dismay that the visitors had left the city for a village about six miles to the south. But before he could turn his weary camel in that direction, Malchus planted his own overworked beast directly in front of him and refused to budge.

"We are *not* traveling today," Malchus declared flatly. Gaius was startled to see a glint of steel in the eyes of his normally compliant friend.

"What are you doing?" the leader shouted. "Get out of my way! There's no time to lose!"

"The time, O Impetuous One, you have already lost," Malchus replied. "The race, you have already lost to your betters. Your sanity, you appear to have lost between here and Babylon. And your friends, you are about to lose. We go no further this day." He sat like a stone upon his camel, resolute and unmoving. If Gaius were to reach this village today— this place called "Bethlehem"—it was clear he would do so alone.

Gaius looked pleadingly to Blastus, but the exhausted man's sunken eyes and heavy eyelids declared more emphatically than any speech that he would soon be on a bed, not on a journey. The argument, too, was lost. The three friends would spend the night in the city and leave early the next morning for the village. Almost certainly the other Magi would arrive first.

That night while his two friends slept, Gaius fidgeted,

his thoughts tumbling. Trying unsuccessfully to ignore the gusty snoring of Blastus, he walked to the open window of the inn and stared out at the sleeping city. One great star blazed on the southwest horizon…toward Bethlehem. Somewhere, out beyond the city walls, beyond the orchards and fields, three of his countrymen were drawing near to the experience of a lifetime. And a nagging little voice whispered that he might have been among them, exulting and worshiping, had he but quieted his heart to seek the God of Daniel.

"What is wisdom, my brother?" a quiet voice, smooth as olive oil, asked from behind him.

"You tell me, Malchus," Gaius sighed. "I always supposed it meant arriving at the answer before anyone else."

"Indeed?"

"Your tone tells me you think otherwise. Well then, what do you say? What *is* wisdom?"

"As to that, I cannot tell you. But I can tell you this. Seeking is as much a part of the equation as finding. And without the seeking, there is no finding. My heart tells me, Gaius, that this newborn King we have pursued across the world will be mighty in counsel—and dear to the heart of Daniel's God. I do not wish to find Him simply to best my brother Magi. I want to find Him that I might worship and adore."

"Well, you've missed your chance," Gaius declared gloomily. "We've lost. The race is done. The search is over."

Malchus placed a hand on his friend's slumping shoulder. "On the contrary, dear Gaius. The search has only begun. I will seek this King as long as I live and wait for His counsel."

"But He's just a child now. It may take years!"

"Perhaps, my friend. Perhaps. But wisdom is also found in waiting. Now—let's get some rest."

The weary pair stumbled over to their sleeping mats and soon Gaius heard the rhythmic breathing of an exhausted man fast asleep. But he himself could not even close his eyelids. He kept turning over in his mind the events of the past weeks. Had he really been too hasty? Was true wisdom to be found in waiting for the counsel of heaven? Would he and his friends be remembered for their gifts of gold, frankincense, and pomegranates?

As he pondered this, a line from the writings of their glorious forebear, Daniel, leapt to mind. Whether prompted by his late-night discussion or by the mighty star even now blazing over Bethlehem, Gaius did not know. But he could not get this puzzling sentence out of his brain:

Those who are wise will shine like the brightness of the heavens, and those who lead many to righteousness, like the stars for ever and ever.

Gaius wasn't sure to what this prophecy referred, but he desperately wanted to be one of those wise men, and he hungered to lead many to this "righteousness." But how to become such a counselor? How could he hope to shine "like the stars for ever and ever"?

And suddenly he knew. The answer came in a flash as he stared out the window at the star they had followed for so long. Malchus had it right. The answer—no, *all* answers—were to be found in this newborn King of the Jews, who at that moment slept peacefully somewhere only a few miles distant. Gaius turned over and smiled for the first time in months. At last—late but not too late—he understood.

True wisdom was to be found in waiting for the counsel of this King. And if he had to wait a few years to hear this counsel, so be it. He would do so. He might have missed out on being the first foreign dignitary to welcome this great King into the world, but he would not be the last. He would bring his gifts of gold, frankincense, and pomegranates, whether anyone would remember or not.

For Gaius knew he had already received a better gift than anything strapped to the back of his camel. He had been granted a small gift of wisdom—and he knew now where to find more, if only he would wait for it.

As Gaius closed his eyes and drifted off to peaceful sleep, a stray beam from the Bethlehem star seemed to streak through the night skies to caress the sleeping man's cheek. And in those quiet moments another of Daniel's "stars" winked to life.

SEVEN

HE KNOWS ALL

He told her, "Go, call your husband and come back."

"I have no husband," she replied.

Jesus said to her, "You are right when you say you have no husband. The fact is, you have had five husbands, and the man you now have is not your husband. What you have just said is quite true."

"Sir," the woman said, "I can see that you are a prophet."

JOHN 4:16-19

Suppose—for whatever reason—you find yourself in the market for a good counselor.

Your marriage has hit a teeth-jarring stretch of rough road.

Your career path has dwindled to a narrow track—then faded out altogether.

Your joy of living has smothered under an unshakable blanket of depression.

Your kids have taken you to the wall—and halfway through it.

So you pick up a phone book. You start asking around. You quiz your friends. How do you find a reliable someone to help you through a difficult period in your life? What qualities would you look for in a counselor?

Yes, I see that hand. *A good listener,* you say? That's essential, I agree.

Another hand. *Empathy.* Very good. We all want someone who can identify with our hurts and stress.

One more volunteer with an answer? *Knowledge.* Of course. You don't want to go to all the hassle and expense unless you can be assured of an expert who can really help you sort through your problems and leave you with a little hope. Certainly you'd want someone who knows more about the critical issues than you do. Otherwise, why bother?

That final characteristic is key, isn't it?

Every good counselor has to *know* some things. No one trusts an uninformed guide. Put yourself in Independence, Missouri, back in 1850. If you and your family were looking for a wagon train bound for the wilds of distant Oregon, you'd want a wagon master who'd *been there.* You'd want someone with a thorough knowledge of the water holes, the easiest mountain passes, the weather patterns, and the wisdom to deal with hostile Indians.

By the same token, if you're going to make yourself extremely vulnerable to a counselor, trusting that individual with your life direction in a time of crisis, you'd better be sure of his or her claim to specialized knowledge. Many individuals have been taken in by "experts" whose office walls were papered with bogus certifications and phony degrees. Unfortunately, there is such a thing as sham knowledge.

A FOOLISH PROPHET

My mind goes back to a Christmas when I was probably no more than nine or ten. December 25 was rapidly approaching, and my parents had hidden the gifts from the prying eyes of their four children. One day I decided to have some "fun" (that was the plan, anyway) and make the claim that I already knew what presents I'd be getting. I had been reading some silly science fiction novella about mental telepathy and other supercharged powers of the mind, and I suppose I thought I'd see if I had any.

Big mistake.

"So, Mr. Know-it-all, what do you think Mom and Dad are giving you?" asked my skeptical sister.

"A two-way radio," I said without blinking an eye. Now, I had in mind a fancy desk model with loads of dials and gauges and buttons and a whip antenna and a corded microphone. It hadn't occurred to me that I might be getting a green G.I. Joe two-way headset radio—but my sister already knew that's exactly what was waiting for me in a dark closet somewhere.

"YOU PEEKED!" she shrieked, accusing me of one of her own foibles.

"I did not!" I protested, then added, "You mean that's what I'm *really* getting?"

Understand, I honestly never thought I was going to get a two-way radio. I was just being a tease, boasting about my sham knowledge. But my sister was convinced my eyes had wandered where they had no business snooping.

"Okay, so what *else* are you getting?" she demanded, suspicion thick as ice on a Wisconsin pond.

I thought quickly, trying to pick some gift I knew I didn't have a chance of receiving. *Hurry now. What's big, expensive, and way out of reach?*

"An airplane," I replied confidently. But another shriek told me I'd picked the wrong item.

"You DID peek!" my sister accused, wagging her sharp index finger in my bewildered face. "You *did* look in the closet, *didn't* you? *I* got you a model airplane—and I'm not taking it back for something else!" Then she turned and fled, calling out for Mom and Dad to inform them of their youngest son's holiday spying spree.

But it wasn't true.

I never did peek in the closet (despite what everyone in the family came to believe). My claim to special knowledge appeared to be confirmed by my two lucky guesses, but the "knowledge" truly was a sham. And I paid for it.

Sham knowledge can be deadly; I know it surely killed much of my Christmas cheer that year. Sham knowledge gives the appearance of expertise without the reality, the semblance of understanding without the substance. Those who specialize in it try to build public confidence in their abilities by claiming a knowledge they do not possess. Sham knowledge is always dangerous, but perhaps nowhere is it more so than in those we trust as counselors.

And that's why Jesus is so refreshing.

Why? Because His knowledge is real, not sham. Total, not partial. And personal, not indifferent. Our Lord's full knowledge is one big reason we can rightly call Him a Wonder of a Counselor.

THE THINGS HE KNOWS

Just think about what this means. Meditate for a few moments on all the streams of knowledge that Jesus possesses. According to Scripture, He knows (at least) the following:

He knows our thoughts.

Have you ever sat across from someone and found his thought processes utterly baffling? You can see what he's doing and what he's planning, but you have no idea *why* he acts the way he does or says the things he says. From where you sit, his behavior makes no sense. It doesn't add up. You can't begin to understand what's going on in his thoughts.

Jesus can.

He sees our thoughts as easily as we see clouds in the sky.

The Gospels are peppered with some form of the phrase, "Jesus knew their thoughts" (see Matthew 9:4; 12:25; Mark 2:8; Luke 5:22; 6:8; 9:47; 11:17). He knew what His opponents were thinking as well as what occupied the minds of His friends.

Imagine what an advantage that would be for a counselor! We are such broken creatures that often even we ourselves are not fully aware of the wildly mixed messages and half-truths we convey. Our words are shaped, colored, and textured by a thousand emotions, experiences, prejudices, and misunderstandings. Counselors who depend on our words to shape their advice are handicapped from the beginning by their incomplete knowledge of what's truly going on in our hearts.

Not Jesus. He knows our innermost thoughts, even when they remain hidden from us.

He knows our intentions.

The apostle John tells us that people were so impressed by Jesus' feeding of the five thousand that a mob made plans to alter the direction of His ministry. Scripture says that "Jesus, knowing that they intended to come and make him king by force, withdrew again to a mountain by himself" (John 6:15).

Can you imagine what a good counselor might do with such valuable information? If a counselor could reach into an individual's mind and instantly identify his or her hidden intentions—the real, driving motives behind everything else—how might that counseling session change?

Suppose a man made an appointment to see Jesus while secretly intending to participate in a bloody Zealot raid on a Roman outpost. Further suppose that this man came to Jesus hoping for some unintentional encouragement for his plans, but never intending to reveal his true intentions. Jesus, of course, would see right through the smiles and light conversation; he would know before the dialogue began what was really at stake. How do you think His counsel would differ from that of an unenlightened guide? How long would it take Jesus to cut to the chase?

Through His Holy Spirit, Jesus is still giving out wise counsel today. And Jesus' counsel can be trusted, for He always deals straightforwardly with our intentions, whether hidden or exposed.

He knows all human hearts, both individually and as a group.
Scripture records that twice Jesus cleared the temple of merchants and moneychangers, once at the beginning of His
ministry and once at the end. John says that after the first
incident, "many people saw the miraculous signs he was
doing and believed in his name. But Jesus would not entrust
himself to them, for he knew all men. He did not need man's
testimony about man, for he knew what was in a man" (John
2:23-25).

In other words, Jesus didn't need to be informed about
the character of any particular human heart nor about
human hearts in general. He "knew all men" and "knew
what was in a man." He didn't need to research the nature of
humankind, nor did He conduct experiments to see what
we're really like. He just *knew.*

Most counselors need months and even years to get to
know their clients—their history and fears and desires and
quirks and hopes—before they can provide any significant
help. Like an onion, we all need extensive "peeling" (with the
accompanying tears) before we reveal our core.

But Jesus cuts through to the core in a heartbeat. At this
very moment He knows you better than does your mother
or father, brother or sister, boss or coworker, spouse or best
friend. He knows you inside out and from top to bottom.
His counsel is tailored specifically to you and is based on His

comprehensive knowledge of every facet of your life—indeed, every cell of your body.

He knows all of human history, from beginning to end.

In one of the most remarkable sermons of all time, Jesus outlined what life would be like at "the end of the age." In the middle of His talk He described a "great distress, unequaled from the beginning of the world until now—and never to be equaled again" (Matthew 24:21).

Wow! How could He make such a statement, unless He knew *everything* about *all* such "distresses" no matter when they occurred (or were to occur), from the time of creation to the time of final judgment?

At that one instant, He could compare the distress of the "end of the age" with the plight of the Armenians in Turkey before World War I, the Jews during Hitler's reign of terror, and the Kosovar Albanians, who were driven from their homes by Serbian militia at the close of the twentieth century.

And don't imagine that His comprehensive knowledge of human history was confined to "general trends" or worldwide, cataclysmic events. The Gospels tell us, for example, that Jesus knew precisely who would refuse to believe in Him and who would betray Him (John 6:64). He knew that one of His closest friends would deny three times that he had ever walked with Him (Matthew 26:34). He knew how and when He would die and how and when He would rise again (Matthew 16:21; John 18:4). And He knew the exact hour of His departure from earth (John 13:1).

Can you imagine what a difference such detailed historical knowledge would make to a counselor? He would not have to hedge his bets because of uncertainty about the future. He would not have to guess about where old booby traps might be hidden. He would not have to waste time wondering whether he was getting the full story. He could counsel you with perfect confidence based on perfect knowledge.

That's exactly the kind of counselor we have in Jesus.

He knows human suffering and grief—firsthand.

Some counselors tend to alienate their clientele because they can't make an emotional connection with their patients' pain and suffering. Because they themselves have not endured the agony of an unfaithful spouse or an abusive relative or a wayward child or a chronic disease, they don't know how to empathize with their patients. As a result, they may unintentionally patronize or judge the very ones they are seeking to help and encourage.

That's never been a problem with our Wonderful Counselor, for He was "a man of sorrows, and familiar with suffering" (Isaiah 53:3). He was "oppressed and afflicted"

(53:7) and finally "poured out his life unto death" (53:12) for us. The writer to the Hebrews reminds us that in Jesus "we do not have a high priest who is unable to sympathize with our weaknesses, but we have one who has been tempted in every way, just as we are—yet was without sin" (Hebrews 4:15). He is our brother (2:11) who was "made like his brothers in every way, in order that he might become a merciful and faithful high priest.... Because he himself suffered when he was tempted, he is able to help those who are being tempted" (2:17-18).

In other words, if Jesus were to open a counseling clinic in your hometown, He would not offer you a couch to lie on, but His shoulder to cry on.

Everything She Ever Did

One of my favorite scenes of the Wonderful Counselor at work is painted in John 4, the famous story of the woman at the well. Jesus goes out of His way to visit Samaria, a despised land off-limits to orthodox Jews, in order to strike up a conversation with a notorious local woman. This odd pair begin their dialogue by speaking about water and from there move to religion, history, morality, metaphysics, and eschatology. But the discussion never becomes merely academic; it is profoundly personal throughout.

At one point Jesus tells the woman, "Go, call your husband and come back."

"I have no husband," she replies.

"You are right when you say you have no husband," Jesus answers. "The fact is, you have had five husbands, and the man you now have is not your husband. What you have just said is quite true" (4:16-18).

Did you observe the Wonderful Counselor at work? He knows the woman's thoughts. He knows her intentions. He knows her desires and her struggles. He knows her complete history, though she's never met Him before. And He knows intimately her fears and her long years of suffering.

"Sir," the woman says, "I can see that you are a prophet"—then abruptly changes the subject.

And you know what? Jesus lets her! This Wonderful Counselor who knows all things has no intention of rubbing her face in her sins. He knows this is a woman whose heart can be opened to Him, and He uses His infinite knowledge to lead her to life abundant. One day in heaven we will meet this redeemed woman and hear her describe in person how Jesus "told me everything I ever did" (4:39), lovingly tapping His infinite knowledge to usher her into His kingdom.

Jesus' memorable encounter with the woman at the well proves that He is far more than a Master of Information. He is infinitely more than a Pharaoh of Facts or a

Sultan of Statistics. He is our Wonderful Counselor who knows how to use His infinite knowledge to lead us to life indeed.

Worth Waiting For

Just three Christmases ago I was a longtime bachelor, wondering if I'd ever marry the woman of my dreams. I was pretty sure I had met her—we'd started dating in March and I was convinced by October—but by December the fires had started to wane. It wasn't that I'd discovered qualities in her that I didn't like or that we just couldn't get along. No, the longer I saw her the more I liked what I saw, and the more time we spent together the more I loathed being apart.

The problem, quite frankly, was that she didn't feel as I felt. "At least, not yet," she'd coyly declare.

This reluctant vision of loveliness had invited me to her parents' home to celebrate that Christmas, and both the invitation and the holiday presented me with a dilemma. How could I properly express my interest in a woman who might never return my love?

For weeks I'd thought about buying her a fine string of natural pearls, but her pointed hesitance to repeat those magic words, "I love you," caused me to waver. Should I make such an extravagant purchase for someone who might not appreciate the sentiment? Would such a gift be a cause for celebration or embarrassment? Perhaps I ought to get something else—maybe a less-expensive strand of cultured pearls? Or possibly I shouldn't join her for Christmas at all?

I struggled over what to do, first leaning one way, then the other. And it wasn't the choice of gift that caused me so many sleepless nights; my real struggle was over the decision I thought I'd soon have to make regarding our relationship. Was this going anywhere or not? I'd made my intentions clear enough, but still she insisted she wasn't ready. Should I go for broke, buy the expensive pearls, and hope for the best? Or should I throw in the towel, get something less precious (translation: a lot cheaper), and ride off alone into the sunset?

One night while pouring out my heart in prayer, telling the Lord of my dying hopes and increasing anxiety, He seemed to speak directly into my mind. I "heard" eight clipped words, distinctly, although not audibly. It startled me, for in my life God had never done such a thing before (and never has since). I've been a Christian since I was four years old, and although I've probably asked for such a direct communication countless times, never before had my request been granted. This time, though I hadn't even asked for a special word from heaven, I got it.

Just wait a little longer. She's worth it.

No promise of a wedding in spring. No guarantee of a sweet "I love you." No assurance that my affection would ever be returned. Only, "Just a wait a little longer. She's worth it."

I bought the pearl necklace. Not the cheap one, but the one that tweaked my bank account. We celebrated Christmas at her parents' home. We had a wonderful time.

She still didn't say "I love you."

But seven months later to the day, I discovered just how much Jesus knew that night He counseled my wavering soul, "Just wait a little longer. She's worth it."

You've never seen such a beautiful bride.

Lisa, my love, you truly are "worth it"! And I'll be forever grateful that our Lord is not only a Wonderful Counselor who knows all things, but also a Mighty Fine Matchmaker. You're the best Christmas present I've ever unwrapped in July.

S.H.

EIGHT

HE LISTENS

In my distress I called to the LORD,
and he answered me.
From the depths of the grave I called for help,
and you listened to my cry.

When you entertain thoughts of God, what sort of thoughts are they? Do you normally picture Him speaking…or listening?

I'd be willing to bet that most of us picture God as speaker, not listener. We're probably nudged in that direction by good, biblical phrases such as "the Word of God" and "thus says the Lord."

But like any great counselor, God is not only an insightful speaker, He's also a world-class listener. He not only gives sound advice and wise counsel, He first listens—really listens—to the deepest cries of our heart.

Jesus Christ—Emmanuel, God with Us—is a phenomenal

listener. Perhaps you've never thought of Him in those terms. But it's true. Our Wonderful Counselor demonstrated this habit repeatedly during His earthly ministry.

Remember how intently Jesus listened to the two confused disciples on the road to Emmaus just days after His crucifixion? Luke says that the two men "were talking with each other about everything that had happened" when Jesus came up and began to walk alongside them. The pair were somehow prevented from recognizing Him, and after a few moments Jesus asked, "What are you discussing together as you walk along?" (24:13-17). The downcast disciples stopped dead in their tracks and replied, "Are you only a visitor to Jerusalem and do not know the things that have happened there in these days?" (24:18).

"What things?" Jesus asked (24:19). (Good listeners ask good questions.) With that open invitation, the two men poured out the whole amazing story—a story Jesus, of course, knew far better than they themselves. The three of them walked seven miles together along the road, the two disciples talking and talking, and the Stranger listening to every word (24:20-24).

That's my favorite way to listen. I can get a little antsy sitting in one place for an extended time. For my money, there's nothing like hashing over nagging worries and perplexities on a long walk through the countryside. Larry, my coauthor, agrees, and we've had some excellent walks—swapping concerns and spinning long-range strategies. Not long ago, a dear friend of Larry's lost his father after an agonizing, messy illness. Larry and his friend were going to meet for coffee, but decided instead to take a long walk through the back country southeast of Portland. Larry's friend just needed to talk, and he poured it out, mile after mile along those graveled roads. He went through the details, the worry, the fear, the shock, and the grief. The sun slipped low on the horizon as the miles slipped by. Cattle and horses grazed in emerald green meadows and the waning light of the October sun cast long shadows across the road. Larry's friend didn't see a bit of it—nor did he require Larry to say much. He knew Larry cared, knew he was really listening, and knew he had permission to talk it all through. So that grieving man just unloaded all the churning thoughts that had gripped his insides for days.

It was the same—and even more so—on the road to Emmaus.

WHY WOULD HE DO THAT?

The two men who walked the road that day had endured an even greater trauma and shock than losing a family member. This was their *Lord* who had been seized and executed by the

Romans. Their fondest hopes as well as their deepest affections had been centered in Him. They had a lot to work through!

Yet we often miss all of that when we read Luke's account. The story has become so familiar and well known through the ages that we have ceased to marvel at what it teaches. Have you ever stopped to really ponder the profound mysteries here? Consider just a few:

- Why would God deliberately keep these good men from recognizing Jesus?
- Why didn't Jesus immediately identify Himself?
- Why did Jesus ask these followers—not once but *twice*—about what they were discussing, since He plainly already knew the answer?
- Why did Jesus remain silent as these troubled men recited their version of His crucifixion and rumored resurrection?

On the surface, our Lord's actions that day don't seem to make much sense—especially if we suppose that the main goal of communication is to relay bits of information. If we imagine that Jesus is basically a Divine Mouth, then what He did that afternoon remains cloaked in mystery.

But what if our Lord is much more than a wise speaker? What if He also knows the value of attentive silence? When we recognize that Jesus is our *Counselor,* His actions that day make perfect sense. Any counselor worth his salt knows he must work hard at listening, at trying to "hear" the feelings behind the words. One expert in the field writes, "Counselors who talk a lot may give good advice but it is seldom heard—and even less likely to be followed. In such situations counselees feel that they have not been understood. In contrast, listening is a way of telling a counselee, 'I care.'"[1]

That is precisely what Jesus was doing that day on the road to Emmaus. He was telling two deeply discouraged disciples, "I care. I care enough to listen to your doubts, your disappointments, your confusion. I care enough to ask you how you're doing. I care enough to keep silent when it's best to do so. And I care enough to give you My full attention, without any distractions getting in the way. I love you, and so I listen."

We've all had conversations with someone who only pretended to be listening. Oh, he'd occasionally grunt or give some generic response like, "I see," to show he was "listening"—but you knew very well his mind was elsewhere. Or maybe it was a woman, eyes darting all over the room to see who might be approaching. Your friend might have been fac-

---

1. Gary Collins, *Christian Counseling, A Comprehensive Guide* (Waco, Tex.: Word, 1980), 27.

ing you and standing in proximity to you, but something told you that he or she was really more interested in some other problem or situation—miles and miles away.

Perhaps you had difficulty as a child getting your parents to listen to you. How frustrating that can be for a little one! Chuck Swindoll used to tell a story about his young daughter rushing into his office and spilling out some concern in a big jumbled rush. The good pastor stopped his daughter and asked her to calm down and speak more slowly.

"Then *listen* slowly, Daddy!" she blurted.

Dr. Swindoll realized with a start that he had been treating his little daughter impatiently, cutting her off or walking away before she had finished what she wanted to say. So she felt she had to rush—while she still had her daddy's attention. It was a strong reminder to sit still, give eye contact, and let his girl have the time she needed to speak her heart.

If we're honest, most of us will admit to wondering if God Himself might be reacting in a similar way. Right? His eyes are invisible to me; are they focused on my eyes as I speak…or wandering around the universe? His expression is invisible to me too. Is He interested, engaged while I tell Him my hurts and concerns…or masking impatience and boredom? Oh yes, He certainly hears me, because He is all-powerful and all-knowing. But…would He really rather be somewhere else when I pray? Could He be more interested in one of the zillion other prayers that pour into heaven in the same instant?

Sometimes, we feel we have to tell Him something over and over again, just to make sure we "get through." We act like Ralphie Parker, the rosy-cheeked little boy in the 1983 movie *A Christmas Story* who desperately wanted "a Genuine Red Ryder Carbine Action Two-Hundred Shot Lightning Loader Range Model Air Rifle." Ralphie took every opportunity he could—with his parents, with his teacher, with Santa—to make known his all-consuming desire. He repeated himself endlessly and gave as many "hints" as he could think of, all because he wasn't sure anyone was truly listening.

Have you ever played the part of Ralphie in your relationship to God? I have. I've worried that He wouldn't really hear me. After all, He has a universe of distractions to vie for His attention: a volcanic eruption on Mars, an exploding star in the Orion belt, a meteor shower on Jupiter. Or maybe He's deep in thought over how to avoid a crisis in Madagascar, or preoccupied with more "important" people who alter the destinies of untold millions by flipping the levers of government or big business.

How could He be expected to find time for little me?

Christmas brings us the good news that God can be expected to, because He has told us to expect *exactly* this.

When David says in Psalm 40:1, "I waited patiently for the LORD; he turned to me and heard my cry," he means that God bent low to catch every agonized syllable. He means that his Lord deliberately turned His ear toward David to hear not only his words, but the pain and passion beneath and around and between the words. The *King James Version* translates this verse more literally, "I waited patiently for the LORD; and he *inclined* unto me, and heard my cry."

In biblical times people were said to speak to each other's ears; to listen closely they "inclined their ears." To incline one's ear means to pay close attention to what is being said, "as if to catch the faintest sigh."[2] And to think that God Himself declares that He bows down His ear to hear every whisper of prayer uttered by the least of His distressed children!

More Than a Good Counselor

Good counselors *listen*—and in Jesus we have not just a good counselor, not just a great counselor, not merely an extraordinary counselor, but (as Isaiah says) a *wonder* of a counselor. Jesus delights to incline His ear to us so that He may hear

---

2. Robert Jamieson, A. R. Faucet and David Brown, *Commentary on the Whole Bible* (Grand Rapids, Mich.: Zondervan, 1961), 422.

every sentence, every word, every syllable, and even every unformed moan that escapes our lips. "We do not have a high priest who is unable to sympathize with our weaknesses," the writer to the Hebrews reminds us, "but we have one who has been tempted in every way, just as we are—yet was without sin. Let us then approach the throne of grace with confidence, so that we may receive mercy and find grace to help us in our time of need" (4:15-16).

These verses, please remember, are talking about *you*. It is you He wants to listen to. It is your voice He wants to hear. Don't deceive yourself into believing these words are "for somebody else." The Son of God, the Creator of the Universe, is waiting at this very moment to hear *you* pour out your soul. Are you worried about some disappointed expectation or a cherished hope deferred? At this very instant, Jesus is inclining His ear to you. He is listening for your voice, waiting to hear from you.

You can be sure that your Lord has some wise counsel for you this Christmas season. But perhaps He is waiting to reveal that counsel until He first hears, from your own mouth, about your hopes and challenges and dreams and fears.

Your Wonderful Counselor's door is open. And His ears are all yours.

S.H.

NINE

SIMEON'S SONG

Simeon took him in his arms and praised God, saying: "Sovereign Lord, as you have promised, you now dismiss your servant in peace. For my eyes have seen your salvation, which you have prepared in the sight of all people, a light for revelation to the Gentiles and for glory to your people Israel."

LUKE 2:28-32

I'd be the first to admit that I don't have a great voice. No one has ever asked me to sing during synagogue services, and—well, I don't expect an invitation anytime soon. Who wants to listen to an old man croak out a raspy tune on his ancient and frayed vocal chords? Better leave that to the younger generation.

Still, I *can* sing when the Spirit moves me. Like that day not so long ago in the temple courts. I sang that day. My, how I sang! I tell you, it was impossible for me to keep quiet. The song *had* to get out! If you had been in my sandals, you would have done the same thing—no matter what kind of odd looks people gave you. That's one of the advantages of being old. You stop worrying about what people think of you. You have nothing to prove and no one to impress.

But look, here I am running ahead of the story. I seem to do that a great deal these days. Why don't we start from the beginning?

For as long as I can remember, I've been waiting. Waiting for God—bless His holy Name—to move again in power among His people. Waiting for Him to turn the hearts of Abraham's children back to righteousness and godly devotion. Waiting for the restoration of Israel. And most of all, waiting to look with my own tired eyes upon the Lord's Messiah, who will surely bring all of this to pass.

Messiah! The Coming One...*who has now come!* (Ah, Simeon, Simeon, can you not restrain yourself to tell a story from beginning to end?)

One day many years ago my waiting became more hopeful—and yet still more intense—as I prayed and confessed my sins and the sins of my people. In one extraordinary moment, the Sovereign Lord spoke to my heart. Don't look askance at me, my friend. It was not the fevered dreams of an old man. It was real. As real and solid as the pillars of the temple.

How did He speak, you ask? What did He sound like? Now as to that, I can't say that I'm sure. I can't say it was an audible voice, but neither can I say it *wasn't.* Whatever it was, in that instant I knew with absolute certainty that the Almighty King of the Universe was making a promise to *me,* Simeon of Jerusalem, that I would not be gathered to my fathers before I had seen the Lord's Christ.

Now…can you begin to appreciate what might cause an old man to sing—right out loud? To dance with bent and bowed legs—slow as a grasshopper on a cold morning? I could hardly believe it. What a promise! What unexpected hope! God's pledge moved me to the depths—but at the same time struck fear into my heart. Yes, fear! Who was I, and what was my father's house, that I should receive such a mighty word from the Blessed One? How had He noticed me, from among all the teeming thousands of Israel's faithful? Who is Simeon? A common sheep in the Lord's wide pastures. And why should He so honor me before the scribes and Levites and priests and synagogue rulers? I have read in the scroll of the Lord that "the eyes of the LORD range throughout the earth to strengthen those whose hearts are fully committed to him"—but I never dreamed that those holy eyes would focus upon *me.* In my most fervent dreams, it never entered my mind that the Holy One of Israel would not only see my heart but speak to my soul! Yet that is exactly what He did—with God as my witness, I do not lie.

At first I expected that He would fulfill His promise

immediately. The next hour, the next day, the next week. I wonder how many of the prophets thought the same. Perhaps, my friend, you have encountered something similar in your life, eh? Perhaps you can identify with old Simeon. You know in your heart that God has spoken to you about this or that, and you are leaning on the assurance of His Word…but time drags on. As Moses taught us, the days quickly pass, and we fly away. You know what I mean, yes? You expect the answer around the next corner, but life leads on from corner to corner and the answer remains hidden in the counsels of heaven.

That's how it was with me. I believed His word, but my oh my, I'm not Methuselah! I don't have the length of years of father Adam. As the days and weeks and months fled by, I saw nothing but more wrinkles on my weathered face and more hesitation in my slow gait. My eyes were growing so dim, I wondered sometimes if I ought to remind the Blessed One to bring Messiah *very near* when He brought Him!

As it happened, He did just that. But I will speak of that in a moment.

Deep in my heart, I knew I had nothing to fear. No, not in the slightest. Yes, I had grown old and my body weary— but I had received the promise of the Sovereign Lord! *I would not die until I saw the Lord's Christ!* A man can live a long time on the promise of God. And even if I caught a glimpse of Him on my deathbed, as I was drawing my last breath, I would die a happy man.

Year after year, so it went. I found myself in the temple courts, gazing at young men as they walked to and fro. *Which one? Which one?* Sometimes I felt like Samuel of old, who looked upon Eliab and said, "Surely the LORD's anointed stands here before the LORD."

Like Samuel, I suppose, I couldn't help but look for a kingly brow, a set of square shoulders, or some otherworldly reflection in a man's eyes. *Which one, Lord? Is it him? Or him? Will it be today?* I saw hundreds of noble, majestic faces on the strong sons of the blessed in Israel. But *Him* I never saw.

Until that day.

Until the day I sang!

It began like any other day. I roused my aching bones from my battered sleeping mat, rose slowly, and reached for a worn cloak to warm myself against the early morning chill. And I prayed as I always did: *Sovereign Lord, could this be the day? Might these old eyes look today upon the Consolation of Israel?* I heard no reply—again, as other days. As I went about my morning duties, my thoughts never ventured far from the hope deep in my heart, lodged like an arrow.

Toward late morning I felt…something. (How feeble words can be at times to tell the way of it.) A nudge. A tug. At the same moment, I knew the Spirit was upon me, moving me, just as the silver-green leaves of an olive tree rustle in a strong east wind. No, I heard no voice and no scroll fell from the sky, yet I suddenly felt a tremendous desire to enter the temple courts. Don't misunderstand: I love visiting the temple and I spend a great deal of my time there, but this was…*different.* Something from outside myself both pushed me and pulled me toward the temple.

I couldn't resist it.

I didn't want to.

As I hastened through the narrow, noisy streets of Jerusalem, I pondered what might be awaiting me. *Is there a message from the Sovereign Lord that I must hear? Am I to be sent somewhere? Could I be about to learn where I might see the Lord's Christ?* But this made no sense to me. *Why wouldn't the Lord just tell me, as before? No, this must be something else. I must hurry. Move, you old legs, stir yourselves! The Holy One of Israel bids you to His house!*

"Hurry" is a relative term for a man my age, but I made haste after my fashion to reach the temple courts as quickly as I might. As I turned the final corner, I looked up from the street…*and there He was!*

I suppose I'd tried to imagine that moment seventy-times-seven through the long years. But in all my ponderings and fancies, I had never imagined it like this.

There were no square shoulders, no princely brow, no manly beard.

It was a baby.

But there was no doubt. I knew it immediately. I needed no voice from heaven, no prophet's declaration. I knew instantly *this* was the prophesied One. And hear me, dear listener, hear what an ocean of blessing poured down on old Simeon. I went over to His mother, spoke to her, and then *cradled the Messiah in my own arms.* The tears flow to speak of it. I *held* Him! The Savior of the world, God's light to the Gentiles, the Consolation of Israel.

That's when the song came.

It rose in my throat. I could no more have stopped it than the Jordan at flood stage. I sang out as the sons of God must have sung at the creation of the world: loud, lusty notes of praise to God for His limitless grace and goodness. I didn't care a fig for the Pharisees and teachers of the law who shot me disapproving glances. The truth is, I hardly noticed them. What did I care if the high priest himself glared at me—with King Herod over one shoulder and the emperor over the other? Do you understand me? I held *God* in my arms! My mind raced with promise after promise from the scroll of the Lord, as if my soul were being filled to the brim with torrents of heavenly wisdom. Chief among them was this from the prophet Isaiah:

Nevertheless, there will be no more gloom for those
who were in distress. In the past he humbled the land
of Zebulun and the land of Naphtali, but in the future
he will honor Galilee of the Gentiles, by the way of
the sea, along the Jordan—
The people walking in darkness
	have seen a great light;
on those living in the land of the shadow of death
	a light has dawned. (9:1-2)

Do you see why I sang that day? Can you understand
why I praised my God in raucous, joyful song? O, you would
have sung too, as I did: "My eyes have seen your salvation,
which you have prepared in the sight of all people, a light for
revelation to the Gentiles and for glory to your people
Israel!"

As I said, a man can live a long time on the promise of
God. But a man can live best on the song of God!

I know that my days in Israel grow short. My body grows
feeble, and the light has nearly gone from my eyes. But my
heart remains full of song, for I have seen the Light of God. I
know that He will cause the ascent and fall of many in Israel,
and that evil men will rise to oppose Him. But what will this
accomplish? Only this: His light will shine into their dark

hearts to reveal the gloom within. He will remain our Light forever and ever.

That is why I sang that day. And that is why I will continue to sing until the moment of my last breath.

Blessed, final note!

TEN

"DO WHATEVER HE TELLS YOU"

Oh, the depth of the riches of the wisdom and knowledge of God!
How unsearchable his judgments,
and his paths beyond tracing out!
"Who has known the mind of the Lord?
Or who has been his counselor?"

ROMANS 11:33-34

*T*ake her *hand?* What kind of baby did she think I was? At four years of age, I felt more than old enough to keep from getting lost in the Christmas-shopping mobs of downtown Beloit, Wisconsin. I'd just stay close to Mom, keeping within arm's reach of her long winter coat. Yeah. Now *there* was a sensible plan.

And what freedom! After slithering out of her grip I scampered over to one shop window to admire the bright display—lurching, animated Santa, busy elves, and feeding reindeer, all hard at work getting ready for the Big Night. And would you look at those *toys?* Medieval castles, complete with sword-wielding knights and catapults that really fire and siege towers with boarding ramps. The LEGOs! The Tinkertoys! The model ships and planes and tanks! The games! For a long time I drank in this high-octane Christmas vision.

When at last I returned from the North Pole, I thought, *Boy, Mom should see this.* I turned around, spotted her familiar coat, worked my way over to it, looked up—and quickly yanked back my hand when the face of a stranger appeared where my mom's should have been.

My, what a start! Instantly I scanned the crowds for the Real Mom. But somehow she was nowhere to be seen. Not by the bus stop. Not by the store windows. Not waiting on the corner. Where in the world had she taken herself? It didn't seem possible, but...Mom had *disappeared.*

What to do? I didn't panic, but I did recall some other counsel my mother had given me—counsel I decided (this time) to follow. "If you ever get lost," she had instructed, "look for a policeman. He'll help you. He will have on a blue uniform, wear a hat, and carry a gun." I greedily searched the area and in moments located just such a person. I ran over to him, tugged on his crisp blue trousers, and announced, "My mom's lost."

Before I knew it, I was riding in the back seat of the officer's police car (shotgun chained to the front dash), heading for the station. One double scoop ice-cream cone and an hour or so later, I was reunited with my two frantic parents. As they entered the station, I was sitting on a desk, happily listening to a description of how the police radio system worked. I distinctly remember glimpsing the anxious faces of my parents and thinking, *I wonder what happened to them? They look so worried.*

I learned that day that it's never wise to disregard the counsel of someone who knows more than you do, especially if that person also has the benefit of many times your experience and loves you more than words can say.

THE GREEN BEAST

But let's be honest here. While I just wrote, "I learned that day," that's not completely true, is it? It would be more accurate to say, "I *began* to learn that day." Many times since then I have unwisely disregarded the counsel of parents, friends—and most disastrously, Jesus Christ. Although He is the Wonderful Counselor and offers to give me His counsel without limit or charge, I have often disregarded it in favor of my own. This is one lesson I seem destined to keep learning my whole life.

For example, everyone who knows me can tell you that I'm no auto mechanic. In my teen years my dad tried to interest me in basic car maintenance, but I was more interested in playing basketball. So why, about a dozen years ago, did I imagine I could provide a decent home for a green '67 Thunderbird that needed paint, a windshield, a new vinyl top, and a replacement muffler? What made me think I could fix its burned-out turn indicators, replace its worn out turn-signal switch, and refurbish its collapsing headliner? Maybe it was the $650 price tag. Who can resist a steal?

Despite my friends' warnings, against my better judgment, and in defiance of that still, small voice, I snatched up the wreck. Before then, I'd always wondered what it would feel like to be on the busy Sunset Highway in the middle of rush hour when your car conks out.

Now I know.

I sat in the left-hand lane (the "fast" lane) for about fifteen minutes before I managed to restart the beast and creep along at three miles per hour toward the exit on Canyon Road. I called a friend, he picked me up, and the next day he diagnosed the problem: a defective $2.60 fuel filter. After this simple repair the car purred, but doubts began to arise. *I don't like green cars. I don't like Fords. What else is wrong?* The next day we rolled up our sleeves (well, okay, my friend did) and tried to fix the car's brakes, which always felt mushy and never "caught" immediately. He installed a master cylinder repair kit, which improved performance—but it still wasn't right. Heedless, I took the T-Bird seventy miles to the beach.

Just before I arrived, the engine started clanking. But what could I do? I proceeded to the coast, took a long walk on the sand, then returned home, my noisy ride clanking all the way. When I finally checked the oil level, I discovered it had disappeared. Nothing on the dipstick. Nothing at all. But where could it have gone? I could detect no leaks or burning. I replaced the oil and hoped for the best.

The following Wednesday, at work, someone knocked on my office door and asked, "Is that your car that's leaking gas in the parking lot? The smell is real strong."

I needn't have looked. Of *course* it was my car. A multi-colored gas film, floating on large puddles of rainwater, sur-rounded my poor vehicle. I looked under the chassis and saw a pinprick stream of gasoline pouring from the tank. While someone from the warehouse fetched a tub to catch the leak-ing gas, I caught a ride to a nearby automotive store to buy some glop for repairing the hole. Several hours later, at 5 P.M., I turned my sweater and pants inside out (to keep from staining them) and walked outside to work on the wounded car. But when I opened the sealed package I discovered the glop had cemented itself to its paper wrapper. Frustrated, I begged another ride back to the automotive store, got a replacement, and as I was leaving, a young guy and his girlfriend yelled out from across the shop, "Hey! Did you know your pants are inside out?"

There's more to the story, but I trust you get my point. I ignored the counsel of friends, conscience, and my Lord, and ended up exactly where I never wanted to be.

WHERE ARE YOU?

How about you? Where are you on the learning scale? Have you mastered this critical lesson? Or are you just beginning your course work?

Part of our trouble, I think, is that often our Lord's counsel just isn't what we expected:

He counsels us to wait when everything within us wants to *act*.

He challenges us to give a chunk of money to meet a need, when we wonder how the bills will be paid next month.

He nudges us to speak to a certain individual about faith in Christ, when that person seems like the *last* man or woman on earth who could be interested in a spiritual message.

He asks us to step up and take on a task we know very well exceeds our time, experience, and abilities.

So very often, His counsel just doesn't seem to add up. Who can understand divine math? Who can ace the quizzes when two-plus-two sometimes equals one thousand? According to our careful calculations, our Lord's counsel sometimes makes no sense at all. We run it through the computer and come up with a string of zeros.

More often than we would care to admit, however, we don't accept God's counsel simply because we don't *like* it.

It's not what we want.

It's not what we expect.

It's not what we hoped for.

It doesn't fit into our plans.

We are like a four-year-old boy at Christmastime, rebelling against his mother's counsel to take her hand so that he won't get lost amid throngs of holiday shoppers. Somehow we imagine we have a better plan, so we wind up following strangers' coats, buying green disasters, and causing no end of grief to those we love the most.

The question we all must answer, even this Christmas season, is this: Will we trust our Wonderful Counselor *even when His counsel seems to defy logic and conventional wisdom?* How will we respond when we can't search His judgments or trace out His paths? In the end, will we trust His counsel, or cobble together a life plan of our own?

But It's So Strange!

This is far more than an academic question. And it's much more than a holiday-inspired inquiry. In fact, it goes to the very heart of our walk with Christ. As sure as dandelions sprout from Oregon lawns, this lesson has a way of popping up again and again in the course of our lives.

In both Old Testament and New, men and women from all backgrounds and pedigrees were confronted with the choice of following God's "strange" counsel or trusting their own.

To the wandering Israelites, God said to gather a certain amount of manna for each person, and to eat all of it the day it was gathered. When they did so, "he who gathered much did not have too much, and he who gathered little did not have too little" (Exodus 16:18). But a few who disregarded the Lord's "strange" word stashed away part of their gleanings until morning—and found that "it was full of maggots and began to smell" (16:20).

To Joshua, on the eve of a battle with Jericho, God said, "March around the city once with all the armed men. Do this for six days. Have seven priests carry trumpets of rams' horns in front of the ark. On the seventh day, march around the city seven times, with the priests blowing the trumpets. When you hear them sound a long blast on the trumpets, have all the people give a loud shout; then the wall of the city will collapse and the people will go up, every man straight in" (Joshua 6:3-5). Now, what kind of military sense did *that* make? From what Cracker Jack box did that prize strategy emerge? But General Joshua obeyed the instructions to the letter, and Jericho literally fell into his hands.

To a frightened Gideon, the Lord said he would hand over the hordes of Midian, a belligerent host "thick as locusts" whose "camels could no more be counted than the sand on the seashore" (Judges 7:12). And how would God accomplish this great feat? Not by an Israelite army of 33,000. (That was "too many.") Not to a division of 10,000. (Still "too many.") But to a little band of 300, God said He would give glorious victory. Gideon listened to this surpassingly strange counsel (although not without qualms), and in a few hours saw his enemies completely routed.

To the leprous Naaman, God said, "Go, wash yourself seven times in the Jordan, and your flesh will be restored and you will be cleansed" (2 Kings 5:10). What a bizarre prescription! It was an affront to a man's intelligence! A furious Naaman asked, "Are not Abana and Pharpar, the rivers of Damascus, better than any of the waters of Israel? Couldn't I wash in them and be cleansed?" (5:12). God's counsel seemed nonsense to the powerful Syrian general.

But as long as he refused it, he remained leprous.

As soon as he followed it, he was healed.

The question is simply this: Will we follow God's counsel, even when it seems strange? This appears to be an extraordinarily difficult lesson to swallow, even for those who have walked with God for years. Remember Solomon? Surely he belonged to the "mature believers" group, if anyone did. After all, he'd been raised by the "man after God's own heart," and as a young man, he'd had a personal encounter with the Lord. God Himself had told Solomon, "I will give you a wise and discerning heart, so that there will never have been anyone like you, nor will there ever be" (1 Kings 3:12). What a promise! And all true! Scripture tells us that the son of David became "greater in…wisdom than all the other kings of the earth" (10:23).

But that did *not* mean he was free to substitute his own store of discernment for the infinite wisdom of the Lord. That would be as presumptuous as plugging a couple of rechargeable "C" cells into an outlet, charging them to the max, and then assuming you could personally power Los Angeles.

Solomon drained his own wisdom all too quickly, refused God's out-of-the-ordinary counsel—and ruined a golden era of God's blessing on Israel. Here's how.

God had said explicitly in Deuteronomy 17:16-17:

The king, moreover, must not acquire great numbers of horses for himself or make the people return to Egypt to get more of them, for the LORD has told you, "You are not to go back that way again." He must not take many wives, or his heart will be led astray. He must not accumulate large amounts of silver and gold.

Now, so far as counsel goes, this must have sounded like advice from Mars. What ancient middle-eastern king *didn't* accumulate horses and wives and silver and gold? After all, that's what kings *did*. Solomon must have thought so, too, for he pursued them all with abandon.

Solomon accumulated chariots and horses; he had fourteen hundred chariots and twelve thousand horses, which he kept in the chariot cities and also with him in Jerusalem. The king made silver as common in Jerusalem as stones, and cedar as plentiful as sycamore-fig trees in the foothills. Solomon's horses were imported from Egypt.... [He] loved many foreign women besides Pharaoh's daughter—Moabites, Ammonites, Edomites, Sidonians and Hittites.... He had seven hundred wives of royal birth and three hundred concubines. (1 Kings 10:26-28; 11:1,3)

Apparently, it seemed foolish to Solomon to follow God's counsel.

- God said, "Don't collect horses, and especially don't go down to Egypt to buy any." Solomon said, "Doesn't make sense to me," and stockpiled the best Egyptian horses he could find.

- God said, "Don't put together a harem, and especially don't marry anyone from the pagan nations surrounding you." Solomon said, "Thanks, but no thanks," and made as many political alliances as possible through a series of marriages to foreigners.

- God said, "Don't hoard silver and gold." Solomon said, "Must not apply to me," and accumulated vast stores of both, so much so that all the household articles in his palace were made of pure gold "because silver was considered of little value in Solomon's days" (10:21).

Imagine that. Even the wisest man in history—a man who gained that wisdom from God Himself—acted no better than the worst fool in history when he trusted himself and turned away from the counsel of God. Scripture tells us:

As Solomon grew old, his wives turned his heart after other gods, and his heart was not fully devoted to the LORD his God, as the heart of David his father had been. He followed Ashtoreth the goddess of the Sidonians, and Molech the detestable god of the Ammonites. So Solomon did evil in the eyes of the LORD; he did not follow the LORD completely, as David his father had done (11:4-6).

THE FLIP SIDE

That's what happens when we turn away from the wisdom of the Wonderful Counselor and instead trust our own. But, oh, how different it can be when we refuse to rely upon our own wisdom (and sometimes our senses) and instead follow the counsel of God! When we consider the experiences of Joshua, Gideon, Naaman, and others, the payoff is abundantly clear.

"You will find a baby wrapped in cloths and lying in a manger," said the angel to some stupefied Bethlehem shepherds (Luke 2:12). Yet shrugging off the strangeness of the counsel, the shepherds went—and "returned, glorifying and praising God for all the things they had heard and seen, which were just as they had been told" (2:20).

"Put out into deep water, and let down the nets for a catch," said the Lord to a group of tired and disgruntled fishermen (5:4). Despite the absurdity of the instruction, the men did as they were told—and "caught such a large number of fish that their nets began to break" (5:6).

"Do not take a purse or bag or sandals; and do not greet anyone on the road," said Jesus to seventy-two recruits (10:4). Despite the Spartan nature of the counsel, they followed their Lord's instruction—and all seventy-two "returned with joy" (10:17).

And it doesn't stop there.

"Get up! Pick up your mat and walk" (John 5:8). The paralytic did so, and was healed.

"Go, wash in the Pool of Siloam" (9:7). The blind man agreed and received his sight.

"Take away the stone" (11:39). The men obeyed, and Lazarus was raised to life.

"Throw your net on the right side of the boat" (21:6). The disciples followed through and got a phenomenal catch.

"Do not leave Jerusalem, but wait" (Acts 1:4). The early church said, "Yes, Lord," and experienced Pentecost.

It's a lesson repeated everywhere in Scripture and everywhere in our lives—and yet we strain to learn it well. How much better would we fare if only we settled the matter once for all: *No matter how strange the instruction or how odd the counsel, if it comes from the Lord, it is wonderful counsel indeed.*

Of course, it's another thing to discern what is and what isn't His counsel. People have done some pretty outlandish things while claiming "God told me to do it"! In the next chapter we'll explore a bit about how to discern the genuine voice of God. But for now, let's at least make up our minds that when God's Word gives us counsel, we'll follow it, come what may.

THE WISEST COUNSEL OF ALL

Mary, the mother of our Lord, must have mastered this lesson by the time her Son began His public ministry. Both she and Jesus were invited to a wedding where the wine ran out before the end of the celebration—a major *faux pas*. Mary approached her Son about this embarrassing situation, then she directed the household servants toward Jesus and gave them the wisest counsel any of us could ever receive: "Do whatever he tells you" (John 2:5).

And what did He tell them? Frankly, His counsel must have seemed more than a little odd. "Fill the jars with water," Jesus commanded. They did so, then the Lord directed them to "draw some out and take it to the master of the banquet" (2:7-8). Now remember, the feast suffered no shortage of water, but of *wine*. Yet Jesus had these servants lugging massive jugs of water around the grounds.

Strange counsel? You bet.

But these were wise servants. They knew Mary had said, "Do whatever He tells you," not "Do whatever He tells you *that makes sense*." Despite Jesus' strange instructions, they followed His counsel to the letter—and in doing so became instrumental in supplying the host with the best wine of the feast. In fact, the master of the banquet called the bridegroom aside and said of this water-turned-to-wine, "Everyone brings out the choice wine first and then the cheaper wine after the guests have had too much to drink; but you have saved the best till now" (2:10).

This Christmas season let's make our own celebrations "the best" by following Mary's advice regarding her Son: "Do whatever He tells you." Sure, we can rush out to buy some cheap wine (or bargain eggnog) if we so choose.

But why would we, when the best stuff can be had for the price of tap water?

S.H.

ELEVEN

SEEKING GOD'S COUNSEL

I will instruct you and teach you in the way you should go;
  I will counsel you and watch over you.

PSALM 32:8

*J*esus *is* a Wonderful Counselor, and getting a five-fingered grip on that truth opens the door to real comfort in uncountable life situations.

But if we're honest, sometimes there's just a little problem with that arrangement. Sometimes His counsel seems hardest to find just when we need it most.

Why is that? James tells us that our God dispenses His wisdom "generously to all" (1:5)…yet it rarely arrives according to our expectations or timetable.

Take last Christmas season, for example. The two of us had been running a fledgling literary business we called

Crown Media, Ltd. We had great fun and camaraderie in our venture, but toward the end of last year our workload began to dwindle. What started as a flood had become a trickle. And bills were coming due.

Both of us prayed often and diligently that the Lord would guide our business and steer us toward the "right" projects. But weeks turned into months, and still our path for the new year looked no more clear. We asked that God would open or shut doors, that He would direct our steps, that He would make it plain where we were to invest our energies. But for the longest time we could detect no answers to our prayers, no clear counsel to light our way. And yet at that very time we were writing the devotional you hold in your hands about the glories of Jesus, our Wonderful Counselor.

What gives? If His counsel is so wonderful, why does it sometimes seem so hard to come by?

FOUR GENERAL GUIDELINES

Why don't we always see or discern God's counsel? Could it be that we don't recognize it when it arrives? And if that's true, why should this be? I suppose there are many reasons, but rather than focus on the negative, let's consider the positive. What can we do to discern God's counsel for our lives?

1. Be prepared for a varied delivery system.

Sometimes we fail to discern our Lord's direction because we look for it in the wrong places. We keep checking at the front door, but it's waiting at the back door…or tapping gently on a windowpane. We imagine that it must arrive in a certain form or in a familiar way, and we are unprepared to accept the package that actually comes.

God never falls into a communications rut. He's never stuck with just one delivery service. In fact, He will speak to us in many ways through many means, circumstances, and individuals. Through the pages of the Bible, He employs a startling diversity of methods and voices to deliver His thoughts, intentions, and warnings. He has spoken through dreams, visions, prophets and prophetesses, and angelic visitations. He has employed ghostly handwriting on the wall, a burning bush, a towering cloud, and even the vocal chords of a donkey to get His message across.

Consider the wide variety of ways God delivered His counsel to the main characters of the very first Christmas. He instructed and taught and counseled them all in the way they should go, but He refused to deliver His counsel in a single, uniform way.

With Joseph, Mary's betrothed husband, He used Dream Express. On two separate occasions, God sent an angel who appeared to Joseph in a dream. The first time He counseled Joseph not to be afraid to take Mary as his wife, despite her out-of-wedlock pregnancy; the second time He warned him to take his young family and flee to Egypt to avoid the bloodshed ordered by the murderous King Herod.

With Mary, our Lord's human mother, He began His communication with Angel Express. The Lord dispatched the angel Gabriel, not in a dream but in person. Gabriel told Mary that she was to bear the Savior of the world. Immediately afterward, the Lord followed up with Woman-to-Woman Express. Mary traveled to see her relative Elizabeth, who was experiencing a miracle pregnancy of her own. For three months Mary lived with Elizabeth—and who can imagine that she didn't receive some godly counsel while lodging with this godly lady? Next, Mary and Joseph were compelled to travel to Bethlehem by Emperor Express. The Roman emperor Caesar Augustus ordered his subjects to check in at their hometowns, thus unwittingly engineering the fulfillment of Micah's prophecy: "But you, Bethlehem Ephrathah, though you are small among the clans of Judah, out of you will come for me one who will be ruler over Israel, whose origins are from of old, from ancient times" (5:2).

To the shepherds, He sent a singing telegram. An angel of the Lord arrived in the middle of the night with counsel on how to locate and adore the newborn King. He was followed by a vast host of angels, filling the Judean night with joyous declarations of God's goodness and glory.

To Simeon, He spoke in a couple of ways. First, He gave the godly old man an understanding through Scripture about "the consolation of Israel," the coming Messiah. Sometime later He personally revealed to Simeon that he would not die before he had seen the Lord's Messiah. And on the day this promise was to be fulfilled, the Holy Spirit counseled Simeon to visit the temple courts at just exactly the right time.

To the Magi, He somehow revealed (perhaps through the influence of the ancient prophet Daniel) that the preeminent King of the Jews was to be born. He then counseled them to find this King by following a mysterious "star" in the heavens. Once in Jerusalem, the Wise Men were counseled to go to Bethlehem by the priests and teachers of the law, who in turn had been counseled by the prophecy of Micah 5:2. And once their visit was over, the Magi were counseled by God in a dream to return to their homeland by a different route, thus avoiding another meeting with Herod.

That's a lot of counsel, delivered in a multitude of ways:

- Through dreams
- Through angels
- Through Scripture

- Through physical phenomena
- Through a close family relative
- Through Bible scholars
- Through a high-government official
- Through the leading of the Holy Spirit

The truth is, our Divine Counselor never limits Himself to one mode of communication. He guides and directs us through any number of means, according to His sovereign pleasure.

Even today, we'd better be alert to the means His Spirit may be using to answer our prayers...or we may miss the message! When we try to restrict His options of delivering counsel, we cut ourselves off from the guidance and instruction He intends to give us.

Imagine a son away from home for the first time, on a faraway college campus. He's homesick, discouraged—and broke. His parents try to send him encouragement in various ways: funny cards in the mail, a balloon bouquet from the local florist, and even a check for spending money via UPS overnight service. But the son says, "My parents never send me e-mail. I've told them how to do it, but they just won't. That's how I really want to receive mail. I won't accept anything else."

How foolish that would be. The son would be refusing encouragement, fellowship, news from home—and even pocket money!—by insisting that his parents have only one communication option.

Regardless of the "wrapping" or "envelope" in which God's counsel arrives, one thing remains unchanged: It always comes to us with His intensely personal stamp. A literal rendering of Psalm 32:8 might be: "I will give advice *with My eye upon you.*" Our Lord's eyes are locked upon us in a fixed, eternal gaze of love. His counsel always reflects His deep, personal concern for us. And never will He deliver that counsel with the slightest hint of disinterest or apathy.

2. Realize that His counsel is often veiled.

One of the harder Bible truths to embrace is the declaration that our God sometimes veils both His presence and His intentions. Isaiah says it boldly: "Truly you are a God who hides himself" (Isaiah 45:15). Proverbs 25:2 declares simply, "It is the glory of God to conceal a matter." The psalmists often struggled with this difficult fact, as the following verses testify:

- "Why, O LORD, do you stand far off? Why do you hide yourself in times of trouble?" (10:1)
- "How long will you hide your face from me?" (13:1)
- "Why do you hide your face and forget our misery and oppression?" (44:24)

- "How long, O LORD? Will you hide yourself forever?" (89:46)

The Lord Himself admits that He sometimes chooses to speak in ways that seem dark, puzzling, and hard to understand. When He wanted Aaron and Miriam to realize that He spoke in a special way to Moses, He said, "With him I speak face to face, clearly and not in riddles" (Numbers 12:8)—implying that with most others, He spoke enigmatically and in puzzles.

It is no surprise, then, that when we come to the New Testament and the ministry of Jesus, we find the Son of God speaking in parables to crowds that often missed His point. It's no accident that one of the most repeated sentences in the Gospels is some version of, "But they did not understand" (Mark 9:32; Luke 2:50; 9:45; 18:34; John 8:27; 10:6; 12:16; 20:9).

The disciples themselves were troubled by the obscure speech often falling from the lips of their leader. They once asked the Master, "Why do you speak to the people in parables?" (Matthew 13:10).

Jesus answered:

The knowledge of the secrets of the kingdom of heaven has been given to you, but not to them.

Whoever has will be given more, and he will have an abundance. Whoever does not have, even what he has will be taken from him. This is why I speak to them in parables: "Though seeing, they do not see; though hearing, they do not hear or understand." (13:11-13)

Our Lord told parables as a means of winnowing out the hardhearted, to separate those with a genuine interest in God and His program from those without it. His parables often puzzled everyone who heard them; it was a listener's response that revealed the contents of his or her heart. Those who earnestly wanted to know God and follow Him would pursue the matter until they gained a proper understanding of the mysterious lesson (Luke 8:9), while those who had no genuine interest in the things of God would simply drop it and leave (John 6:60-66).

Why should we think the nature of God's counsel would be any different for us than it has been for His people throughout biblical history? If He spoke in parables and riddles and puzzles and unclear speech to men and women in both Old and New Testaments, using this means to separate "the sheep from the goats," then why should we think it strange that He continues to use this method? Today, like then, those who really want to know His counsel will ask and keep on asking; they will knock and keep on knocking; for they know that "everyone who asks receives; he who seeks finds; and to him who knocks, the door will be opened" (Luke 11:9).

It often takes real effort to recognize and understand the counsel of our Lord. The old Puritan John Flavel rightly said, "There are difficult passages in both the works and Word of God." The good news is that those who really want to know and follow His counsel will surely gain the desire of their hearts.

But it may take some time.

3. Don't make unclear what God has already made plain.

The sad truth is that we may even "misunderstand" God's counsel when He speaks in a perfectly clear and understandable way.

About halfway through his gospel, Mark records that Jesus began to teach His disciples that "the Son of Man must suffer many things and be rejected by the elders, chief priests and teachers of the law, and that he must be killed and after three days rise again." Mark emphasizes that "He spoke plainly about this" (Mark 8:31-32).

So how does Peter, the leader of the Twelve, respond? "Peter took him aside and began to rebuke him," Mark says (8:32).

Now, Peter didn't misunderstand His master's words; he

just didn't *like* them. He didn't misconstrue the message; he simply wasn't prepared to accept it. And therefore Jesus reproved Peter sharply: "Get behind me, Satan! You do not have in mind the things of God, but the things of men" (8:33).

How often have we gotten ourselves into trouble because we disliked the plain, obvious counsel of God? "Do not be a man who strikes hands in pledge or puts up security for debts" says Proverbs 22:26, but we did it anyway—and lost a small fortune. "Do not be yoked together with unbelievers," says 2 Corinthians 6:14, but we did it anyway—and married into a lifetime of regret.

Often our Lord's counsel is as plain as can be, but still we don't seem to "get it." Whether we stubbornly misinterpret it or disdain it, however, the outcome is the same: disappointment and defeat.

Be sure of this: While we may sometimes struggle to discern God's counsel for our lives, we never have to wonder whether He might, in some particular instance, set aside or violate the word He already gave us in the Bible. That will *never* happen.

"The grass withers and the flowers fall, but the word of our God stands forever," proclaims Isaiah (40:8). "God is not a man, that he should lie, nor a son of man, that he should change his mind. Does he speak and then not act? Does he promise and not fulfill?" declares Moses (Numbers 23:19). "I tell you the truth, until heaven and earth disappear, not the smallest letter, not the least stroke of a pen, will by any means disappear from the Law until everything is accomplished," insisted Jesus (Matthew 5:18).

The long and short of it is that because "Jesus Christ is the same yesterday and today and forever" (Hebrews 13:8), He will never counsel us to do that which His Word prohibits, nor will He instruct us to refrain from what the Scriptures urge us to do.

He will never counsel a man to put together a shady business deal.

He will never counsel a woman to get a divorce just because she's unhappy.

He will never counsel a believer to avoid serving in a local church.

He will never counsel a boy to dishonor his parents.

He will never counsel a girl to cheat on a test.

Jesus will never counsel you to do anything His Word has already condemned, nor will He ever advise you to refrain from doing what the Bible has already commanded.

Of that you can be absolutely sure.

The key to discerning God's counsel seems to be not only *understanding* that counsel, but *desiring* it—whatever it might be. When our hearts seek to follow God's Word as much as our minds hope to comprehend it, we'll be getting close to the real treasure.

4. Remember that personal discovery often cements our grasp of His counsel.

There is something about personal discovery that flips on crucial circuits in our brain. We can hear a lesson a hundred times, but until we discover for ourselves what it's all about, it remains "locked up." God understands this about the way we're built, and so He designs object lessons that make something in our minds go "click."

Consider the apostle Peter. Although he had been at the forefront of the glories of Pentecost, preaching to multitudes and seeing thousands come to faith in the Lord Jesus, he still didn't understand that God wanted to offer His salvation to the whole world, Jews and Gentiles alike. Now, God could have appeared to Peter in a dream or a vision and told him plainly, "Peter, the gospel is for the whole world, for both Jews *and* Gentiles. So preach to everyone you meet, regardless of their ethnicity." But that's not what He did.

Instead, He got Peter good and hungry, sent him up on a hot rooftop to pray, and put him into a trance. There he showed him a vision of a sheet let down to earth by its four corners, full of all kinds of ceremonially "unclean" animals. "Get up, Peter. Kill and eat," said a voice (Acts 10:9-13). The proper Jew Peter was horrified. "Surely not, Lord!" he cried. "I have never eaten anything impure or unclean" (10:14). To which the voice replied, "Do not call anything impure that God has made clean" (10:15).

This strange scene repeated itself three times, then Peter woke up, confused. What did it mean? While he was puzzling about it, a few men from Caesarea arrived to ask the apostle to return home with them so they and their Gentile friends could hear some message he was to give. Peter immediately left with the men and on arrival in Caesarea spoke with a Roman named Cornelius, who explained why he had sent for the apostle (10:16-33).

And just that quickly, the lights went on.

"*I now realize* how true it is that God does not show favoritism but accepts men from every nation who fear him and do what is right," Peter declared (10:34-35, emphasis added). At last he comprehended the meaning of the strange vision. He was not to consider these Gentiles "unclean," but was to explain to them fully the Good News of Jesus.

Discovery helps us learn, and surprise helps us remember. Both are often-used tools in the arsenal of the Wonderful Counselor.

WAITING AND TRUSTING

Do you need the counsel of Jesus Christ today? Where do you most require His guidance? Is there some area of life where you ache to see the words of Psalm 32:8 fulfilled, some issue where you've been pleading for God to put into action His promise: "I will instruct you and teach you in the way you should go; I will counsel you and watch over you"?

If so, there may be no better "pre-guidance" counseling than the words of Isaiah 8:17, which says, "I will wait for the LORD, who is hiding his face from the house of Jacob. I will put my trust in him."

That's what the two of us did last Christmas season, when we grew uncertain about the direction of our little company. Eventually, the Lord counseled Larry to return to his former job as an editor inside a publishing house. And He counseled Steve to stay where he was. It all came down to waiting and trusting, the common denominator of divine counsel.

Waiting and trusting. It was the same leading up to the very first Christmas, wasn't it?

The Jewish nation waited long centuries for its Messiah to arrive.

The Magi waited two years before they beheld the King of the Jews.

Mary waited nine months to hold her promised Son.

They all understood, as we must, that on this earth waiting and trusting always go hand in hand. It may be hard at the time, but when at last we look at the bright present opened before us—when waiting and trusting have given way to having and enjoying—then we will know beyond all doubt that His guidance is worth waiting for and His counsel deserves our full trust.

Even if we don't "get it" right away.

TWELVE

THE COUNSELOR'S QUESTIONS

When he was twelve years old, they went up to the Feast, according to the custom. After the Feast was over, while his parents were returning home, the boy Jesus stayed behind in Jerusalem, but they were unaware of it. Thinking he was in their company, they traveled on for a day. Then they began looking for him among their relatives and friends. When they did not find him, they went back to Jerusalem to look for him. After three days they found him in the temple courts, sitting among the teachers, listening to them and asking them questions.

LUKE 2:42-46

I never did like the kid. Not from the moment I laid eyes on him.

Something about the way he carried himself brought the bile into my throat. I don't know how to describe it. Outwardly humble, yes, but—no peasant boy should have that sort of self-assurance. *Who did he think he was?* The way he just walked in and made himself at home—it wasn't proper, I tell you, no matter how impressed some of our elders might have been with him.

This penniless lad off the streets breezed into the temple courts one day after the Feast and *took a seat among us.* This I saw with my own eyes. I am not jesting! He acted...well, as if he *belonged.* I didn't pay much attention to him at first; I suppose I thought he was delivering a message to one of the elders.

Of course, I am almost always in the temple courts, along with my father and brothers and my soon-to-be father-in-law. A long time ago my parents arranged for me to marry into one of the powerful families of Jerusalem—a wealthy, politically connected group with strong leanings toward the Sadducee point of view. Although my father-in-law—it's hard not to speak of him in that way, even though Tabitha and I are only engaged—was deposed by the Romans a couple of years ago, everyone knows that he still runs things around the temple. He has five strong sons—they're here every day too—and everyone just naturally assumes that each of us will have a turn at the top.

The point is, we're here day after day, doing our civic and spiritual duty and earning the trust of the people, all from the ground up. Everyone knows us. Everyone respects us.

Everyone realizes God has chosen *us* to lead the people. Everyone greets us with deference in the marketplace, which is only as it should be. And when we speak—Ah! Lesser men cover their mouths and strain to hear each word.

It's quite a responsibility, I can assure you. But our family has always borne it well. Were it not for the Gentile dogs who rule us from Rome, who knows what we might have become?

Now…what was I saying? Oh yes. Common folk fall silent when we speak—knowing who we are, of course—and strain themselves to see who can sit closest to our inner circle.

But not *him!* It was clear from the beginning that he just didn't understand. And as I said, he certainly didn't belong. His clothes, for one thing—homespun peasant rags with the stench of Galilee hanging heavy on them. He didn't even know who we were! Or at least—he didn't seem to care. He sauntered into the temple courts that day and immediately took a seat as close as he could get to the scribes and teachers of the law. He claimed he had reached the required age for Torah instruction, so we couldn't throw him out…but I ask you again, *who did he think he was,* taking a seat so close to our deliberations?

That would have been appalling enough, but of course, the impudent child didn't leave it there. Oh yes, he did sit quietly for a long time, listening to the elders explain the intricacies and secrets of Moses' Law. I almost forgot about the little intruder for a time.

And then—the *nerve!*—after a brief pause in the lecture, this ignorant peasant boy opened his mouth and *started asking questions!* Can you *imagine?* This nobody from Galilee—I've since learned he's from Nazareth, that stinking, thief-ridden village to the north that isn't even *mentioned* in the Torah. What good could possibly come from *there?*—invites himself to our holy gathering, takes up space more suited to his betters, and then has the temerity to start asking questions of the most learned scholars in Jerusalem.

To this day, I can't get over the fact that the elders didn't shoo him out of the room. For whatever reason—you explain it, *I* can't—the elders decided to tolerate this peasant boy and even humor him. Now, to be fair-minded about it, his questions sounded decent enough. The elders and scholars seemed pleased, even delighted, with many of them. But I ask you, who is this…this *Nazarene*…to open his mouth AT ALL in our presence?

While I might grant that the child was a good listener and asked the occasional apt question, he completely lacked an observant eye. I sat not twenty paces distant from him, but he never *once* seemed to notice my scowls or my obvious demonstrations of disapproval. He never picked up on even one of my many silent suggestions that he accept his place and keep his mouth shut.

No, it was as though *I* were the irrelevant one in that gathering! For hours on end, he just kept posing questions and listening to the answers.

What *kind* of questions, you ask? By the Scrolls! How can you expect me to remember the exact words of an unlearned, insignificant peasant boy? There were so *many* questions!

Very well, very well…out of courtesy and to illustrate my point, I'll try to remember some of them. I think many went something like this:

"What is the greatest commandment in the Law?"

"Who should be considered my 'neighbor'?"

"What sort of kingdom will the Son of David rule?"

"Who is the "Son of Man" spoken of by Daniel the prophet?"

"What is the proper way to pray?"

"Which is greater, love or faith?"

"How can a man learn to obey God from the heart?"

"How will Elijah the prophet prepare the way of the Lord?"

"Why is it the Lord's will to crush the Messiah, as Isaiah says?"

"Why does David cry out, 'My God, my God, why have you forsaken me'?"

"Why does God say He requires mercy, not sacrifice?"

"What is the best way to use stories in teaching the Law?"

"What does it mean that God is no respecter of persons?"

"Why does God permit that which He hates in order to accomplish that which He loves?"

And so the questions came, in a gentle torrent, question after question after question. My head grew dizzy with questions, and still they came. I thought after the first day that this boy would be drained of his curiosity, but it soon became clear he was just getting started. He came back the second day and asked more of them! The third day the same. Likewise the fourth. I thought it would never end. Where did he eat? I have no idea. It was as though he fed on this discussion of the Word.

The worst part, of course, is that the scribes and elders seemed to *enjoy* his incessant questions, which encouraged the child no end, in my view. I could tell by the way they glanced at one another and muttered among themselves that they were taken with this street child. It was most infuriating. When I would put forward a question or observation of my own, I actually found myself being ignored!

This urchin asked questions about the Law. Questions

about application of the Law. Questions about our history. Questions about contemporary events. Even personal questions that I thought sure would make these wise men squirm. But they didn't squirm; they didn't even frown. They seemed delighted that such a young boy would not only take such a serious interest in the Torah but also in their own lives.

Oh, but *I* saw what lay behind all of these multiplying questions! This dirty little provincial wasn't interested in God's words, nor in the welfare of God's servants. No! He wanted only one thing: to be at the center of attention, to be praised for his "precociousness." I really think he had it in mind to take my place. Imagine such a thing!

By the fourth day I was ready to explode. I began wondering how I could get this infuriating waif thrown out for good, how I could get things back to the way they were, to the way they should be. I was in the middle of one particularly promising scenario when I heard a commotion toward the edge of the crowd, which had grown each day over the week. I looked up and saw a peasant couple, worry in their faces, scanning the audience in front of the scholars. Suddenly the man broke away and made a beeline for this obnoxious boy at the front. The boy never noticed a thing until the man put a strong arm on his shoulder. Then he turned, smiled, and immediately got up and joined this man in a brisk walk back to what obviously was the fellow's concerned wife.

I strained to hear what they said to each other, but all I could make out were two more questions from the boy: "Why were you searching for me? Didn't you know I had to be in my Father's house?"

His *Father's* house?

Just that suddenly they were gone.

I felt exhilarated—but unfortunately, everything in the temple courts did *not* immediately return to normal. For several days the elders insisted on discussing this "unusual" boy and his "insightful" questions. You will think I exaggerate on this next point, but I swear by the temple, what I say is true. They kept repeating how much his questions reminded them of the questions *God* constantly asks us in His Word. Searching the Scrolls, they reviewed many of those questions from the mouth of the Holy One: "Where are you?" "Why are you so angry?" "What is the matter?" "Who gave man his mouth? Who makes him deaf or mute? Who gives him sight or makes him blind?" "What are you doing here, Elijah?" "What do you see?" "Whom shall I send? And who will go for us?"

The most galling thing was that they actually said this boy would likely make a fine scholar himself someday, a counselor anyone would be privileged to approach. "He listens so intently," they said. "And his questions! What a counselor he will make!" Blah, blah, blah. What a joke!

Soon I'll show everyone that this unlettered peasant boy is nothing. I'm still the young man with promise around here! You'll see! Or my name isn't Caiaphas.

THIRTEEN

INFINITE SUPPLY

The Spirit of the LORD will rest on him—
the Spirit of wisdom and of understanding,
the Spirit of counsel....

*T*wenty years ago it was Cabbage Patch Kids. A few Christmases later it was Nintendo. Sometime after that, Tickle Me Elmo. Then Beanie Babies. Then Furbys. More recently it was Pokémon. What will it be this year, or the year after?

We have no way of knowing what "must-have-it" gift craze will grip America next, but one thing is certain: The media-hyped demand will enormously outstrip the supply. At the very least, the toy's distribution channels will clog up sufficiently to make a lot of holiday shoppers anxious, unhappy—and some of them downright mean.

Bizarre stories abound of normally placid homemakers and cross-stitching grandmothers fighting like fiends in store aisles over the latest must-have toy. When it comes to laying hands on scarce and hotly demanded novelties for dear little Tommy or Tammy, all civility and charm go out the window; it's snarl and scratch, grab and grasp, claw and clutch. Normally courteous neighbors who wave at one another across the cul-de-sac morph into raging WWF body-slammers.

It isn't pretty.

What evil potion turns these tranquil suburban Jekylls into raging Hydes? Simple scarcity. Holiday rampages such as these might remain relegated to the realm of nightmare had the products so maniacally sought been readily available.

Terrible thought, but—could such a thing ever happen in the spiritual realm? Could our demand for the wise and tender counsel of Jesus Christ ever outstrip the supply? With urgent requests continually pouring in from all over the globe, twenty-four hours a day, fifty-two weeks a year (and probably double-time during the stressful Christmas season), do we have to worry about heaven's phone lines becoming jammed...or its channels of distribution becoming overwhelmed?

Most of us probably don't worry about such a curious possibility. But we *do* fret that we won't receive Jesus' abundant counsel when we really need it. We *do* wonder how God's life-giving counsel can make its way to us in our most critical hour of need.

How can we be assured that heaven's precious counsel

will be available when we desperately need it? The Scripture answers with three surpassingly lovely words:

The Holy Spirit.

PROPHESIED, PROVIDED, PROMISED

Nearly eight hundred years before Jesus was born, the prophet Isaiah declared that our Wonderful Counselor would be filled with the Spirit of the Divine Counselor. "The Spirit of the LORD will rest on him," Isaiah predicted, "the Spirit of wisdom and of understanding, the Spirit of counsel and of power, the Spirit of knowledge and of the fear of the LORD" (11:2).

The very counsel of God would be on Jesus' lips, Isaiah said, not only because He would *be* the Wonderful Counselor, but because God's Spirit of wisdom would fully rest on Him. This glorious truth so encouraged Isaiah's soul that at least twice more in his book He made similar predictions:

Here is my servant, whom I uphold, my chosen one in whom I delight; I will put my Spirit on him. (42:1)

The Spirit of the Sovereign LORD is on me, because the LORD has anointed me to preach good news to the poor. (61:1)

Isaiah foresaw a Messiah so brimming over with God's Spirit that He couldn't help but speak out God's divine counsel. And the Gospels leave us in no doubt that the prophet's predictions were amply fulfilled in Jesus.

Matthew quotes Isaiah 42 to prove Jesus' claim to be the Messiah. He writes of Christ, "Many followed him, and he healed all their sick, warning them not to tell who he was. This was to fulfill what was spoken through the prophet Isaiah: 'Here is my servant whom I have chosen, the one I love, in whom I delight; I will put my Spirit on him'" (Matthew 12:15-18).

The apostle John gets in on the act too. He tells us how Isaiah's predictions were gloriously fulfilled in the earthly ministry of Jesus Christ, to whom God gave "the Spirit without limit" (John 3:34).

Just in case anyone might fail to recognize the unique bond between Jesus and the Holy Spirit of God, Luke delights to elaborate on that intimate relationship:

- "Jesus, full of the Holy Spirit, returned from the Jordan and was led by the Spirit in the desert" (Luke 4:1).
- "Jesus returned to Galilee in the power of the Spirit" (4:14).
- "At that time Jesus, full of joy through the Holy Spirit" (10:21).

- "God anointed Jesus of Nazareth with the Holy Spirit and power" (Acts 10:38).

Add to these explicit statements the testimony of all four Gospels concerning the baptism of Jesus, in which the Spirit is said to descend on our Lord in the form of a dove (Matthew 3:16; Mark 1:10; Luke 3:22; John 1:32), and you have extraordinary confirmation of all that Isaiah foresaw.

Okay. That's good, solid biblical teaching.

But how does it help me, right now, with the sticky situations I'm trying to juggle? How does it assure me that the counsel I need from heaven will always be available? The New Testament is only too happy to answer that question.

IT IS GOOD THAT HE WENT AWAY

If we were promised only that Jesus Christ would be our Wonderful Counselor and that He would fulfill His earthly ministry through the power of the Holy Spirit, we would be in trouble.

Deep trouble.

Why? Because Jesus isn't walking around in Judea today. How could we find Him in a moment of crushing need? Where could we access His counsel at those perplexing, sometimes frightening crossroads of life when we don't know which way to turn? Jesus foresaw these concerns clearly, and so declared one day to some startled disciples, "I tell you the truth: It is for your good that I am going away. Unless I go away, the Counselor will not come to you; but if I go, I will send him to you" (John 16:7).

Who was this "Counselor?" And why did the disciples need Him if they already had the Wonderful Counselor? Our Lord had previously explained to His men, "I will ask the Father, and he will give you another Counselor to be with you forever—the Spirit of truth. The world cannot accept him, because it neither sees him nor knows him. But you know him, for he lives with you and will be in you. I will not leave you as orphans; I will come to you" (14:16-18).

Think of what is being said here. Jesus is promising His followers—including you and me—that although He was about to leave this world, He would never abandon us. It is impossible that He should leave behind even a single orphan! Rather, He would certainly "come" to us as often as we might need His counsel. How? Through the Holy Spirit.

This is the same Holy Spirit whom Peter calls "the Spirit of Christ" (1 Peter 1:11). He is the same One whom Luke calls "the Spirit of Jesus" (Acts 16:7). And He is the same Divine Person whom Paul names "the Spirit of Jesus

Christ" (Philippians 1:19). That is why Jesus could say, "The Counselor, the Holy Spirit, *whom the Father will send in my name,* will teach you all things and will remind you of everything I have said to you" (John 14:26, emphasis added). The Spirit testifies about Jesus (15:26) and guides God's children "into all truth. He will not speak on his own; he will speak only what he hears, and he will tell you what is yet to come" (16:13). Most important, Jesus declared, the disciples could trust the Spirit's counsel because "the Spirit will take from what is mine and make it known to you" (16:15).

Strands of deep mystery and profound comfort twine themselves together in these words.

Our Lord Jesus doesn't need to carry a cell phone or wear a beeper at His side to hear our cries for help. His very Spirit lives within us—"closer than hands or feet, closer than breathing." I don't have to wait in line for His wonderful counsel (although I may have to wait for it). I will never be put on hold, transferred to voice mail, routed around the universe by an automated operator, bumped to some bored angel behind a computer, or handed an appointment card for some morning six months hence.

My access to God is instant.

The counsel of Jesus Christ is *immediately* available through the Holy Spirit. Nor will I have to concern myself that my particular problems or needs will draw too deeply upon my Lord's resources.

I will never weary Him with my questions.

I will never exasperate Him with my needs.

I will never tire Him with my calls in the night.

I will never cause Him to pull back from me in the slightest degree.

I will never make Him groan because of my weakness, sigh over my clinging dependence, shake His head in revulsion over my lack of understanding, or pull back in disgust over my wavering faith.

Never! Not in ten thousand lifetimes. In fact, the Bible calls upon us to "pray without ceasing" (1 Thessalonians 5:17, NASB). God would love to keep the line open with us all day long. He would *love* to hear us call to Him all day and cling to Him all night. He would love to hear our voice, hour by hour, minute by minute, from this moment on! And what counsel would await us if we fell upon Him in such a way! What wisdom we would receive if we grabbed hold of Him like Jacob wrestling with the angel!

Our Lord's supply of counsel through the Holy Spirit will forever exceed our demand. If God sighs over anything, it is over the fact that we don't demand enough, that we don't come to Him more often, that we don't cry out more frequently, that we don't patiently wait for His response.

IT STILL WORKS TODAY

What does it mean, in practical terms, to receive Jesus' wonderful counsel through the Holy Spirit? The New Testament gives several examples of how the Spirit gives us the very words of the Wonderful Counselor.

Suppose you are arrested one day for claiming allegiance to Christ. A scary proposition indeed! How will the Spirit counsel you in that hour? Jesus has told you, " 'When you are brought before synagogues, rulers and authorities, do not worry about how you will defend yourselves or what you will say, for the Holy Spirit will teach you at that time what you should say' " (Luke 12:11-12).

Or what if you find yourself embroiled in a debate about the claims of Christ? Should you run home and pull some books off the shelf to arm yourself with the best possible arguments? That's not what Stephen did. When certain "men began to argue with Stephen," Luke says, "they could not stand up against his wisdom or the Spirit by whom he spoke" (Acts 6:9-10).

Nor are such examples of the Spirit's counsel limited to Bible times or long-dead disciples. How many guest speakers have been holding forth at a weekend retreat or a youth rally or a Sunday morning service when, quite apart from their notes, they suddenly hear themselves telling a story or making a point far better than anything they had prepared? And they'll think, *Where did that come from?*

The Wonderful Counselor looks down from heaven with a smile and gently whispers, "Didn't I tell you to expect something just like that?"

Of course, the counsel we receive from Jesus through the Spirit isn't always about what we should say. Sometimes, it's counsel that keeps us from saying anything.

Pastor Chuck Smith tells how he received a difficult call from the wife of a couple he had known and loved for a long time. The woman poured out a heartbreaking story about her spouse, who had taken up with another woman. She told Chuck where this adulterous couple was living and begged him to make a visit. Perhaps he could talk some sense into her straying husband?

Chuck consented and a day or so later set out on his gut-wrenching errand. He had been praying earnestly that God's Spirit would lead him to say just the right thing, to speak some thought or insight that would cut to the heart, convict the man of his sin, and prompt his sincere repentance.

But when Chuck approached the shabby little apartment on the wrong side of the tracks, he wavered. *Could he go through with this?* He knocked and his friend answered, great surprise betraying his face. The pastor asked if he could come in and the shaken man, not knowing what else to do, stepped back from the door and motioned Chuck inside.

As Chuck entered the seedy tenement, he glanced around and noted how much this man had lost. He had been a successful businessman with a fine home in a prime neighborhood where he lived with a beautiful wife and happy, responsible kids. Now, this—dirt everywhere, springs poking out of a fourth-hand couch, threadbare clothes, and a bleak, almost desolate apartment. His friend had lost everything: wife, kids, home, respect. The contrast made Chuck sick to his stomach.

Just then the man's "lover" appeared in a doorway—a woman as frayed and dilapidated as the wretched apartment. At that moment Chuck lost it. Gone were his words of wisdom. Gone was his composure. Gone was his intent to read his friend the riot act.

He simply sat there and wept, feeling like a fool.

Finally, after several long minutes of this blubbering, Chuck managed to choke out a weak, "I'm sorry, I must go," rose, and left quickly.

As Chuck drove back to church, he was certain he had blown his only chance to talk sense into his friend. He knew he'd have to call the man's wife to explain the fiasco, and he dreaded it.

But God had a surprise in store. Shortly after Chuck returned to his office, he received a call. An ecstatic woman was on the line—the friend who had asked him to visit her husband—showering the pastor with joyful thanks. "But I didn't say anything," Chuck protested. How could his contemptible visit have done any good?

Chuck didn't know that silence was exactly what his friend needed. The man had steeled himself against the lecture he was certain to receive—but he wasn't at all prepared for a broken heart and flowing tears. Fifteen minutes after Chuck had fled the apartment, the man came to his senses, realized how much he had lost, repented of his sin, and returned to his wife and family. That home is restored today because of the counsel of Jesus delivered through the Holy Spirit—counsel not through words, but through silence and a weeping, broken heart.

No Delivery Problems

We never have to worry that Jesus might run out of wonderful counsel by the time He gets to us. We never have to fear that something will get gummed up in heaven's distribution channels and prevent His counsel from reaching our ears. We might often wish that our Lord were physically present with us, especially when we cry out for help and assurance, but He has already assured us, "I tell you the truth: It is for your good that I am going away. Unless I go away, the Counselor will not come to you; but if I go, I will send him to you" (John 16:7).

The Counselor has been sent. And He is with us and in us today, relaying His wonderful counsel, exactly as He hears it from Jesus.

You and I can be assured that we will never hear the sort of words that come from weary department store clerks when the rush is on for some must-have toy.

You won't be told to take a number.

You're always first in His affections.

You won't be asked to make another appointment.

The Counselor is in, right now.

You won't walk away empty-handed.

He'll fill you to overflowing.

You won't have to take a rain check.

All He has and all He is are constantly available.

And you will never, never have to accept a substitute.

In fact, there is none.

FOURTEEN

THE (VERY) BEST CHRISTMAS PAGEANT EVER

You guide me with your counsel,
and afterward you will take me into glory.

PSALM 73:24

*T*he first thing you notice are the colors.

Impossible greens.

Reds you can feel with your eyes closed.

Blues that draw you into unchartable depths.

Golds and yellows like an August sunrise on steroids.

Purples so regal the other colors seem to bow in their presence.

All these—and more I can't even put into words—burst from the foundation of the city with the brilliance of a thousand suns. Newcomers generally think they should shield their eyes from its intensity—but soon realize that *nothing* can hurt them here, so they relax and just take it in. Besides, you couldn't pull your eyes away from those colors even if you wanted to (and who would?). All around, everywhere you look, blaze rainbows that have happily ditched every last bit of old earthly coyness.

This place is always achingly beautiful, but did you know it's especially breathtaking during Christmas? I was surprised to learn that they celebrate Christmas here, even as we used to. I always thought this city would have a timeless quality about it, an eternal flavor with no place for clocks or days or months or seasons or years.

But it's not like that at all.

The angels keep patiently reminding me that we've left behind shadows and types—that this is the realm of the solid and real. The days here are *real* days, the seasons *real* seasons—more intense, more palpable, more firm and graspable than anything we ever knew on old earth.

"How could anything here be *less* than what you had there?" an angel once asked me. (Angels are an inquisitive lot…always asking questions.) "Surely you have read in the Book, 'On no *day* will its gates ever be shut'? And haven't you read that 'On each side of the river stood the tree of life, bearing twelve crops of fruit, yielding its fruit every *month*'? We have never lived in some kind of timeless void, drifting aimlessly through unmarked moments without end. So how could we fail to commemorate His Majesty's arrival on earth as Emmanuel? How could we ignore the greatest mystery in the cosmos? And how could *our* Christmas celebrations fail to be more real and joyful and fulfilling than anything the sons and daughters of men dreamed up on old earth?"

The angel's right, of course. While I can clearly recall the tender moments of Christmases past—the candlelight church services, the squeals of delight from children cradling new toy trucks or dolls, plunking coins in the Salvation Army kettles, the lusty singing of ancient carols—I gladly admit that they are as nothing compared to what I've experienced here.

(Ah me! Now I understand how the good apostle John labored so mightily in seeking to describe heavenly realities with weak, old, earthly words. It's like trying to weave a tapestry with reflections and shadows.)

During my last few years on old earth, I witnessed what I thought were two of the most stunning nativity plays I'd ever seen. In the first one, the woman who played Mary radiated such warmth and compassion that she had most of us sniffling by the end of her first scene. And her voice! With tender power she sang the mysteries of her Son's birth, marveling over God's choice that she should bear the Savior of the world.

The very next year I thought the man who portrayed Gabriel must have received some celestial pointers. He seemed to glow with the might of heaven. The director also used real sheep and a horse and a cow to convey the deep humility of the scene. It worked. We really felt something of the sacrifice our Lord made to live as one of us on our poor, wayward planet.

But none of those productions, skillful as they were, could have prepared me for my first nativity play *here.* How can I tell you what swept through my heart when before me stood the *real* Mary, the *real* mother of our Lord, reciting in Aramaic (which somehow I understood) the words of the Magnificat?

And it didn't stop there. In the next scene the *original* carpenter Joseph told us how he was preparing to quietly divorce Mary because of her supposed infidelity, until one night the angel Gabriel suddenly appeared to him in a dream. And *whoosh!* Right before us, the *real* Gabriel appeared, hovering above the stage in glorious heavenly splendor and announcing, "Joseph son of David, do not be afraid to take Mary home as your wife, because what is conceived in her is from the Holy Spirit. She will give birth to a son, and you are to give him the name Jesus, because he will save his people from their sins."

Well, at that point the whole vast audience (about the

size of Alaska) leaped to its feet and erupted into thunderous shouts of "Hallelujah!" and "Amen!" and "Praise and glory and honor to the Lamb!" and a thousand other exaltations I couldn't quite catch. The play had to pause for a few moments as rolling peals of praise rose from uncounted millions of throats and only reluctantly melted away into reverent silence. I think I even saw Gabriel smile a little (though don't tell him I said so).

And can you imagine how I trembled when I witnessed the *authentic* Magi approach Mary to present their gifts of gold, incense, and myrrh? I confess that before then I'd never had a good picture of these exotic Wise Men; I'd always seen them portrayed in clownish costumes, gaudy golden trinkets hanging from their fabric-store sashes. But with a start I realized these men were the genuine articles, regal leaders exuding immense erudition and wealth and power. They explained how they had learned something of the Messiah through the glorious traditions handed down over the ages from the prophet Daniel—the chief wise man of his age, revered by their order—as he ministered faithfully as a captive in the courts of ancient Babylon.

The appearance of the Magi also cleared up another mystery for me. I'd always wondered what sort of "star" guided the Wise Men to our Lord and his mother. Was it a supernova? The unique aligning of some planets? A special, supernatural light in the heavens? Well, today I no longer wonder, for at that moment the *real* Star of Bethlehem suddenly shone overhead, casting its odd light on the holy scene below. Some might ask, "How could you see the star, since it's never night there?" Well, on old earth, did you ever see Venus shining brightly on the horizon some lazy afternoon? That gives only a feeble comparison, but it will have to do. I *can* tell you that this starlight was of a different character from that of other suns—cool, molten silver—and every bit as arresting as it must have been on that dark night over Judea. Like the Wise Men, when I "saw the star stopped over the place where the child was," I also was overcome with joy!

That same jubilant spirit quickly spilled over into the numberless audience—redeemed men, women, and angels alike—and with one voice we all began singing heaven's versions of the carols we had loved all our lives. What a thrill to hear Gabriel and Michael and the seraphim and the cherubim and all the other shining hosts of heaven sing "Hark, the Herald Angels Sing" and "Angels from the Realms of Glory"! Yet I couldn't help but notice how these mighty ministering spirits grew quiet and reflective—almost puzzled, even sad— as the redeemed broke out into another glorious carol:

Thou didst leave Thy throne and Thy kingly crown
When Thou camest to earth for me,

But in Bethlehem's home was there found no room
For Thy holy nativity!
    O come to my heart, Lord Jesus
    There is room in my heart for Thee!

Heaven's arches rang when the angels sang,
Proclaiming Thy royal degree,
But in lowly birth didst Thou come to earth
And in great humility.
    O come to my heart, Lord Jesus
    There is room in my heart for Thee!

That song would have been enough to fill my heart for a million years with a spirit of triumph, but I quickly discovered the celebration was just getting started.

As much as I always enjoyed old earth's Christmas displays, I never dreamed of the light show our Father could put on here! For good reason our brother James wrote, "Every good and perfect gift is from above, coming down from *the Father of the heavenly lights.*" During this whole season, streams of intense, matchless light shine through the foundation stones of our city—jasper, sapphire, chalcedony, emerald, sardonyx, carnelian, chrysolite, beryl, topaz, chrysoprase, jacinth, amethyst—bathing us in brilliant hues that delight our dancing eyes. Combine this bright display with the shimmering light that always fills this place, and it's a vision so lovely you think you can't endure it—but somehow, in God's grace, we've been given the capacity to absorb tidal waves of beauty, and not be flattened.

And then our Father begins handing out presents, much as our brother Paul described: "When he ascended on high, he led captives in his train and gave gifts to men."

From my earliest days of Sunday school, I had always heard that "you can't outgive God," but somehow, I never conceived that such giving might continue into eternity. Much less did I imagine that it would be vastly accelerated! Yet that is the gospel truth. To one man He gave oversight of a star system in the Orion belt; to another He gave a mansion in the Pleiades; to yet another He gave the ability to apprehend His limitless mercy in a whole new way.

And to me?

Ah, how can I tell you of this exquisite gift? If I thought all mysteries would be revealed and all secrets unveiled in this glorious realm, I was both foolish and mistaken. For I know now (by happy experience) the truth of the Book when it proclaims, "No eye has seen, no ear has heard, no mind has conceived what God has prepared for those who love him." Just when I think my God has revealed all of His secrets, He pops out another one to dazzle my wondering eyes!

So what can I do but join the psalmist in declaring, "O

LORD my God, I will give you thanks forever"? There are wondrous, staggering surprises here—and many more, not fewer, the longer we walk these streets of transparent gold! Why, just the other day I ran into Nicholas, the former bishop of Myra. (No one calls him "Saint Nicholas" anymore, since all of the redeemed gratefully wear the title of "saint.") And while I really did find him to be most jolly, he doesn't look a bit "old." In fact, no one here does. Anyway, Nicholas told me he delights in seeking out certain of our redeemed sisters and saying to them, an impish grin on his rosy cheeks, "No, Virginia, there really is no Santa Claus."

But I got the biggest surprise of all just after my encounter with Nicholas. No sooner had I rounded a corner than I observed the longest line of people I had ever seen. It seemed to go on for miles and miles. They were all queued up...to do what? I couldn't quite tell at first—but I admit that my encounter with "Saint" Nicholas did remind me of the long lines I'd seen on old earth when impatient children and their harried mothers clamored to sit down with a red-suited impostor. But *this* couldn't be *that*. So what was it?

I walked to the end of the line and struck up a conversation with sister Natasha, who told me they were all waiting to speak with the Wonderful Counselor Himself. With a twinkle in her eyes she pointed to the front of the line and quoted the gospel: "We saw His star in the east and have come to worship Him."

With a joyful heart I found a place in line and was frankly amazed at how quickly the time seemed to pass. On old earth I had never been in a line a tenth as long as this, but nevertheless I had often lost my patience getting to the front. Not so here! Time is real here, as I said, but it's...well, *different*. The closest I can come to explaining what I mean is that, where on old earth time could seem to drag, here those same times seem to fly. And where on old earth the good times seemed to speed by in a rush, here they linger and lavish us with the richest treats we are capable of enduring. Sorry, but that's the closest I can come. (You'll see what I mean, after you cross over.)

As I neared the front of the line, I received one final surprise: a great Christmas tree standing directly behind the throne of the Lamb. Vaster and more majestic than any old earthly yuletide decoration ever could have been, the tree flamed with light and towered over the cavernous receiving hall. Yet somehow it did not remind me at all of a Noble or Douglas fir or any other of the evergreens I knew from old earth. Instead it drew my mind instantly and inescapably to another tree, to one stripped bare of greenery, where Life gave itself over to death that it might live once more—and us along with it.

As I pondered this great marvel, I suddenly found myself face to face with the Son of David Himself, the Wonderful Counselor and Lord of my soul. I said nothing—I *could* say nothing—but instead stared into His eyes, those deep, fathomless pools of infinite love and wisdom. He smiled a smile that lit my heart on fire and melted my knees and said only this: "Son, I guided you with My counsel, and afterward I took you into glory." He paused, then smiled again and said with a joy that shook the universe, *"Merry Christmas!"*